pastoral
MINISTRY
in the 21st century

the encyclopedia of practical ideas

sermon sparks
worship jump-starts
community service and outreach

foreword by magazine executive editor **Alan Nelson**

Group

Loveland, Colorado
www.group.com

Group resources actually work!

This Group resource helps you focus on **"The 1 Thing®"**— a life-changing relationship with Jesus Christ. "The 1 Thing" incorporates our **R.E.A.L.** approach to ministry. It reinforces a growing friendship with Jesus, encourages long-term learning, and results in life transformation, because it's:

Relational
Learner-to-learner interaction enhances learning and builds Christian friendships.

Experiential
What learners experience through discussion and action sticks with them up to 9 times longer than what they simply hear or read.

Applicable
The aim of Christian education is to equip learners to be both hearers and doers of God's Word.

Learner-based
Learners understand and retain more when the learning process takes into consideration how they learn best.

Pastoral Ministry in the 21st Century
The Encyclopedia of Practical Ideas
Copyright © 2006 Group Publishing, Inc.

Visit our Web site: **www.group.com**

Credits
Editors: Brad Lewis and Carl Simmons
Creative Development Editor: Matt Lockhart
Chief Creative Officer: Joani Schultz
Copy Editor: Mary Ann Jeffreys
Art Director: Kari K. Monson
Cover Art Director/Designer: Jeff A. Storm
Illustrator: Rob Furman
Production Manager: DeAnne Lear

Unless otherwise noted, Scripture taken from the HOLY BIBLE, NEW INTERNATIONAL VERSION®. Copyright © 1973, 1978, 1984 by International Bible Society. Used by permission of Zondervan Publishing House. All rights reserved.

Library of Congress Cataloging-in-Publication Data
Pastoral ministry in the 21st century : the encyclopedia of practical ideas.-- 1st American pbk. ed.
     p. cm.
ISBN-13: 978-0-7644-3153-1 (pbk. : alk. paper)
1. Pastoral theology--Handbooks, manuals, etc. I. Title: Pastoral ministry in the twenty-first century. II. Group Publishing.
 BV4016.P25 2006
 253--dc22
                                      2006002019

10 9 8 7 6 5 4 3 2 1   15 14 13 12 11 10 09 08 07 06
Printed in the United States of America.

Table of Contents

Section 7: Developing Your Leaders and Volunteers

Section 8: Community Service and Outreach

Contributors

The following individuals contributed to the hundreds of great ideas for pastoral ministry in this book.

John Fanella is pastor of Beulah Congregational Church in central North Dakota and the author or editor of more than a dozen books on church ministry. He and his wife, Cheryl, have two children.

David P. Gallagher is senior pastor of Palm West Community Church in Sun City West, Arizona. He's a popular speaker at conferences and a writer of children's, youth, and adult curriculum. He develops practical tools for use in his own ministry, and many of the forms throughout this book and in the Appendix are adapted from tools he created. Dave is the author of *Senior Adult Ministry in the 21st Century* (Group) and *Healing Takes Time* (Liturgical Press).

Joy-Elizabeth Lawrence has lived in seven American states and one Canadian province, attending a variety of worshipping communities. She's a recent graduate of Regent College in Vancouver, British Columbia, with a Master of Christian Studies degree. She and her husband, Justin, live in Grand Rapids, Michigan.

Brad Lewis is contributing editor of REV! Magazine for pastors and was founding editor of Vital Ministry Magazine (REV!'s predecessor). A self-employed editor and writer, he has edited more than 60 books, including four in Group Publishing's Ministry in the 21st Century series. He, his wife, Esther, and their two sons live in Colorado Springs, Colorado.

Jeanette Gardner Littleton is a full-time writer and editor who has served in volunteer and staff positions in the local church, parachurch ministries, and at denominational headquarters. She's edited ministry publications and books, and has written more than 3,000 articles, many for pastors and church leaders. She and her husband, Mark, live in Gladstone, Missouri.

Mark Littleton is a full-time writer and has published 85 books. Mark has served as a youth pastor, Christian education director, and pastor at different times over the past 25 years. He's married to Jeanette and has four children.

Robin Martens has 15 years of pastoral and Christian counseling experience in private practice and as director of Open Door Mission's Christian women's shelter. Robin has extensive biblical training, earned a master's degree in counseling from the University of Nebraska, and is a licensed counselor who also speaks and writes about counseling topics. She lives in Omaha, Nebraska.

David B. Peterson has served in pastoral ministry since 1991. He's now senior pastor of Mountainside Bible Chapel in Schroon Lake, New York, and previously served in a church in New Jersey. Before entering pastoral ministry, David had 15 years of business experience and served in the church as a lay person.

Kristi Rector served as associate editor of REV! Magazine for pastors for six years. She's now copy editor for Group Publishing's three ministry magazines, as well as a freelance writer and editor. She and her husband, Jess, have one child and live in Loveland, Colorado.

Dean Ridings is director of communications for The Navigators, the author of numerous articles and Bible studies, and compiler of *The* Pray! *Prayer Journal* (NavPress). He has a master's degree in communications and a master's of divinity degree. Dean and his family live in Colorado Springs, Colorado.

Kelli B. Trujillo is a writer and editor; she recently co-authored *Jesus— The Life Changer* (Group) with her husband, David. She loves pastors, literally: Her dad is a senior pastor, and David has worked as an associate pastor. Kelli and her family live in Indianapolis, Indiana.

Molly Wright is the director of religious education, pre-K through 8th grade, for St. Thomas More Newman Center in Columbia, Missouri. She also coordinates family ministries, the children's church, and the junior-high service group. She currently serves on the advisory council for Group Publishing's Church Volunteer Central Association.

Foreword

Ideas empower and enable us to do things we could not or would not do without them. Practical ideas—the ones with handles on them, for ease of application—are the useful types. Whether you're Alexander Graham Bell inventing the telephone or Steve Jobs creating a new computer, the implementation of a good idea can help a lot of people.

You're in ministry to help people, to connect them to each other and to God. To do your job well, you need good ideas. Ministry in the 21st century is both very much the same and very different from ministry in the last century. The basic task remains constant: Assist people in their spiritual formation. But new times require innovation. As the rate of change increases, the length of time any one idea will serve us decreases. Therefore, to be effective, we must burn through ideas faster—which means we need to harvest more of them.

You're busy. There's always more ministry than time left at the end of a week. To stay on top of your game, you need to be sharp, stimulated, and constantly equipped with new ideas.

This book is a bonanza of ideas related to pastoral ministry. If you're not the creative type, there's a plethora of succulent, tasty idea treats where the creative process has already been done for you. You'll see things that will make you think, "That's good! I could do that right away."

Even if you *are* blessed with more creative genes, you'll rejoice in a resource like this, because just like Jesus' miracle of feeding the 5,000, you know how one idea can multiply into a lot of other good ones. See this book as a bag of dust to seed the rain clouds of creativity and innovation to get more done in less time, as well as to breathe vitality into programs or processes that have become lethargic from overuse.

Time has a way of making a pastor extremely pragmatic. So let's be honest. Many of the ideas in this book aren't for you personally. You'll quick-read them and say to yourself, "Naw," "Maybe later," or "Tried that." But there will be many other ideas in this volume that will rev your ministry engines. Any one of them will be worth the price of this book, but you've got *several hundred* of them just waiting for you to discover and apply them.

So take this book of ideas, take the ideas you can use here, and take your ministry to the next level. You spend your life helping people know Jesus. We spend ours helping you to be more effective. So go for it!

Alan Nelson
Executive Editor, REV! Magazine

Introduction

Welcome to *Pastoral Ministry in the 21st Century: The Encyclopedia of Practical Ideas*!

We believe that God loves pastors and places a unique call on their lives to serve him and his children in ministry. But we also know that living out the lofty-sounding words in the previous sentence isn't always pretty. Being a pastor can mean working 60-hour, seven-day weeks. Serving can mean "getting your hands dirty" with everything from cleaning backed-up toilets at church to cleaning up the messes in people's relationships. Ministry can mean an endless day where you move from leading a morning Bible study to visiting a dying church member in the hospital to spending all night at a youth group lock-in—and navigating through wildly different emotions at each step.

And we know that you wouldn't trade a minute of what you do. You love being a pastor, and you love the people you serve—even if you could use a little break now and then.

We can't send you on vacation (although we can help you out with a couple of retreats—see page 112). But we *can* help you make it through your day with greater ease. Within these pages, you'll find hundreds of practical, creative, hands-on ideas that you can use in your ministry today. Whether you need inventive ways to prepare to preach, imaginative movie clips that illustrate a sermon point, novel suggestions for getting away with your family, fresh ideas for deepening relationships in your congregation, or innovative ways to make global missions more personal for church members, this book can help. In fact, you'll find more than 600 ideas to help you at work, rest, or play.

TO COPY

Because this book is a collection of practical ideas, we've worked hard to put it together in a practical way. Of course, you can read it from cover to cover if you want. But it's designed to be a reference tool. You might want to start in the Table of Contents, choose a specific area of pastoral ministry where you need tips and ideas, and go from there. Once you get into the various lists of the book, you'll find notes that link you to related ideas. You'll also find ready-to-use forms marked "OK to copy" (look for the logo shown at right) that can help you organize common aspects of pastoral ministry.

As you try the ideas in this book, we hope that you'll discover both new ways to tackle ministry and fresh approaches to the tried-and-true. And we pray that you and your congregation will gain and grow in the process.

May God bless and use you and your ministry!

—Brad Lewis, Editor

Section 1:
Sermon Sparks

Preaching is one of the most important parts of your pastoral ministry. It certainly consumes a good chunk of your time. The goal of this section is to help you put together amazing, meaningful, and powerful content for your sermons. Along the way, you'll also find ideas for making the most of your sermon-preparation time.

Section 1: Table of Contents

22 Great Ways to Start Your Sermons

People often come to church tired, frustrated, stressed out, and even angry. They need a bridge to help them cross from daily life to hearing God's Word. The following ideas for sermon introductions can help provide that bridge.

Dramatic Narratives

With just a bit of creativity and courage, you can use drama to start your sermon.

1. Do a dramatic reading

Choose a contemporary translation of the Bible passage you're preaching on (such as *The Message* or the *New Living Translation*), dim the lights, and read the passage with more emotion and passion than you usually use. Help your congregation to really get focused on God's Word before your sermon has even begun.

2. Pray a dramatic prayer

Create a prayer from your sermon's Scripture passage. During the introduction, dim the lights, have the musicians play some appropriate music, and pray your prayer. If you're not a writer, you'll find a wealth of ideas in *Leading in Prayer: A Workbook for Worship* by Hughes Oliphant Old (Eerdmans Publishing Company, 1995), or in *Grant Us Your Peace: Prayers from the Lectionary Psalms* by David R. Grant (Chalice Press, 1998).

3. Impersonate the author or main character

Let Paul or Joshua or Esther or Job talk directly to your congregation. Cast your sermon's passage in first person and speak to your church in the voice of your passage's author or main character. Don't just recite Bible text while doing this—be as natural and conversational as possible.

4. Impersonate someone who knew the author or main character

Create a fictitious character who might have known or seen the author or main character. For example, you could come to your congregation as one of the Roman soldiers who crucified Jesus, or as a woman in the crowd who saw Moses coming down from the mountain.

An additional benefit of this kind of narrative is that it gives you more "artistic license."

5. Do a contemporary, one-person drama

Recast your sermon's Bible passage to fit contemporary life. Turn Joseph into a modern-day business leader. Turn Nehemiah into a high-rise construction manager. Cast David as the U.S. president or a foreign leader. These contemporary adaptations of Bible stories sometimes provide what people need to identify with them.

Active Learning

Sermon introductions can be more than words. By using active learning experiences, you dramatically increase your congregation's involvement in your sermon and their desire to listen. The more you involve people's senses and the more you make them a direct part of the sermon, the better they'll receive and retain what you say.

6. Give people something to hold

Pass out a prop that matches the theme of your sermon. Then during the introduction say, "I bet you're wondering why you were given a smooth stone when you came in today. Well, today we're going to be talking about God's desire for us to become living stones." An inexpensive, hands-on giveaway helps build curiosity and involves the senses.

CROSS REFERENCE:
For other hands-on giveaways, see Section 4: 20 Worship Service Jump-Starts, beginning on page 90.

7. Give people something to talk about

During your introduction, provide a question for people to discuss for a minute or two with the person next to them. For example, if you're introducing a sermon on facing fear, say, "Share with the person next to you the scariest thing you've ever encountered." After people discuss this for a minute or two, transition back to your sermon by saying, "Whether it was a close call in the car or riding Space Mountain, we've all been afraid. But the Bible teaches us that we can bring all our fears to God and receive his peace."

8. Give people something to do

Get your congregation up and moving, even for just a minute, and you'll dramatically increase their interest in your sermon and what they take away from it. For example, to introduce a sermon on "Bringing Requests to God," say, "You received an index card when you came in. As the music plays, take a moment to write down one thing you'd like to see God do in your life. When you finish, bring the card to the front and place it in this basket." When your congregation finishes this simple yet moving activity, say, "What we've done today is what God wants us to do *every* day. We can always bring our needs before him, and place them at his feet."

9. Give people something to share

Encouraging interaction is a great way to introduce your sermon and to build community. Provide an item that individuals must exchange with someone else during your sermon introduction. For example, give each person a cloth bracelet (something that can be written on with a marker), and instruct people to write their names on the bracelets. Then, to introduce a sermon on "Praying for One Another," ask people to get up, walk around the auditorium, and find others to give their bracelets to. After a few minutes, bring the congregation back together and say, "To help us pray for one another, for the next week, wear the bracelet you received and pray for that person throughout the day."

Stories, Quotes, and Questions

Stories, quotes, and questions in the introduction help connect your sermon to real life.

10. "Survey *says*...."

Conduct a few anonymous interviews during the week and include responses in your introduction. Your *Family Feud* introduction might sound like this: "Eight out of 10 people that I talked to this week said they would never jump out of an airplane without a parachute. The other two clearly didn't understand the question. Trust is hard for most of us, yet God asks us to trust him without hesitation."

11. Use a velvet hammer

Find a light, whimsical, or even comical story to tell before transitioning to a weightier topic. Softening the blow often raises receptivity.

12. Share a personal anecdote

Tell a story from your personal life. This helps listeners identify with you as a fellow pilgrim. Of course, be sure your story relates to the theme of the sermon.

13. Ask a relevant life question

Start a sermon on prayer with a question like, "What activities do you think most strengthen the family?" Then say, "Among all the possible answers, praying together is the most important thing you can do to strengthen your family." Even if people aren't excited about hearing about prayer, most want to know how to strengthen their families.

14. Quote a well-known person

In your sermon introductions, quote from contemporary and familiar movies, athletes, musicians, authors, and Christian communicators. Avoid quoting historical theologians or scholarly authors that people might not recognize.

15. Use statistics, but sparingly

Statistics bore many people, especially when pastors use them to beat up on congregations. Saying, "Two-thirds of churchgoers give less than 1 percent of their income to church" is a path to disaster. Instead, find regional or local statistics to help people think about possibilities instead of shortcomings. The above statistic could be replaced with, "The median income of our county is $34,000. Just think what churches could accomplish if people gave just 5 percent of that to their local church." When using statistics, think local, brief, and positive.

The Element of Surprise

When you do something out of the ordinary—whether it's a minor change or something completely out of character—it instantly changes the whole tone of your sermon. Try the following ways to surprise your congregation during a sermon introduction.

16. Change positions

If you typically preach standing up, sit on a stool. If you usually preach behind a pulpit, come down and stand on the floor in front of the platform. If you normally preach after congregational singing, preach before the music.

17. Change your style of clothing

Dress casually if you typically wear a suit (or vice versa). Put in your contacts if you normally wear glasses when you preach. Or wear an unusual item that relates to your sermon.

18. Invite a special guest to appear during your introduction

An outfitted carpenter might walk up while you're preaching on "Building up One Another," or a uniformed football player shows up when you're preaching on "Putting on the Armor." Talk with these guests for a minute or two. Ask questions that relate to your sermon, such as, "What are the secrets of building something that lasts?" or "What would happen if you forgot your shoulder pads?"

19. Arrange for a "surprise" interruption

Arrange for someone to call on your cell phone during the introduction to a sermon on "Listening for God's Answers." Or have the ushers turn out the lights to introduce a sermon on spiritual blindness. Or arrange for someone to throw a paper ball at you and shout as you're introducing a sermon on dealing with criticism.

20. Use a different format

Invite the pastor of another church to team-preach with you on the theme of church unity. Introduce the idea of an echo sermon, telling the congregation that whenever you say a certain phrase, they should answer with a specific response. For example, during a sermon on God's strength, each time you use the phrase, "I shall not be moved," the congregation responds, "The Lord is my rock and my fortress." Give the congregation the chance to echo at least 10 times during the sermon.

Humor

Humor is another great tool for introducing sermons. Humor allows people to let down their guard, and it introduces Christian joy into the hearts of hurting people. Use these basic principles when using humor in your sermon introductions.

21. Select short jokes with clear punch lines

If you tell a long joke with a foggy punch line, you'll probably get one courtesy laugh from the back row. If a joke is more than two or three sentences, it's probably too long for the pulpit. Use humor to undergird your introduction, not as the *whole* introduction. Begin with a serious statement, then tell a joke or humorous story to illustrate the topic. Remember: You're not a stand-up comic. You want to be a conveyer of truth who uses humor as a tool.

22. Use jokes related to your topic

Unrelated jokes just seem weird. Also, many jokes cross the boundaries of decency and respect. If a joke requires belittling someone—especially in the areas of ethnicity, sexuality, or physical appearance—it's just a cheap joke and isn't true humor. Instead, think of a joke as an illustration that lets you bridge immediately from the punch line to the sermon.

12 Ways to Develop Sermon Illustrations and Stories

Good public speakers are usually storytellers. Mix in personal or universal anecdotal stories as a means of capturing and holding your congregation's attention. People sit up and listen intently when a speaker says, "For example, just the other day I..." or "Maybe this story will help illustrate what Scripture says here."

Use the following ideas to develop stories for your sermons. (To help you keep illustrations and other elements of your sermons organized, see the "Scripture Passages and Illustrations" form on page 19.)

Storytelling Techniques

How can you use storytelling techniques in your preaching? Here are several guidelines.

1. Stick to basic structure

Nearly every story has three elements: beginning, middle, and end (or punch line). When you use a story in your sermon, think in terms of beginning, middle, and end. Catch, hatch, and latch with a story.
- Catch: Get your listeners' attention.
- Hatch: Open the egg and help your listeners see the life within it.
- Latch: Finish with a punchy last line or two.

In addition, make each story brief, direct, and memorable. As a result, your listeners will head home intent on retelling your stories, and they'll recall your whole message because of the stories within it.

2. Paint with vivid strokes

In your stories, seek the right word or phrase to describe what you're talking about. Similes and metaphors are among the tools you'll use to describe what you're saying in vibrant detail. "Eyes like saucers." "Ears like bagels." "His coat hung on him like a dishrag." The more vivid the picture, the more your listeners will remember.

3. Think character

Think about the people in the story. What is this main character like? How can I best describe his or her personality? Make the characters in your stories live in the minds of the listeners. What images come to mind when you hear these names: Captain Ahab? Ebenezer

Scripture Passages and Illustrations

Church Name:

Year:

Date	Service or Special Event Scheduled	Scripture Passages	Illustrations

Scrooge? Scarlett O'Hara? Indiana Jones? These characters live in our minds because their original authors painted them vividly.

As you develop characters in your stories, help your congregation feel something real and deep about them. When speaking of people in Scripture, give them qualities that will make them live in the hearts of hearers. For example, is your Moses more like Charlton Heston or *The Prince of Egypt*? What do your Joseph and Mary talk about as they journey to Bethlehem?

Where to Find Stories

How do you get stories? How can you develop fresh, new, and exciting material? Consider these ways to find and develop your stories.

4. Don't forget biblical stories

Remember that most new material is really old material. Don't overlook the Bible as a source for illustrations. Chances are, a lot of people in your congregation haven't heard biblical stories, even if they've been Christians for a long time. And you can frame even the most familiar stories in contemporary language to help them come alive.

- The Prodigal Son (Luke 15): Tell it as a modern story about a runaway.
- The Good Samaritan (Luke 10): Try it with an unsavory well-known movie character as the hero.

Even straightforward storytelling can be effective. For example, the story of the temptation in the garden (Genesis 3) shows how easy it is to be deceived by Satan, while Jesus' temptation (Matthew 4) illustrates the right ways to battle temptation.

5. Take lesser-known stories and use them in your message

To illustrate friendship and loyalty, consider the story of Mephibosheth, Jonathan's son, whom David befriended after Jonathan was killed. Or tell about Deborah and Barak, the story of how a woman became a prime leader of ancient Israel.

You can also take well-known stories (Cain and Abel, the Tower of Babel, David and Goliath) and dramatize them with fictional details to make them more real to listeners. Describe what the characters look like. Give a few details of dialogue. And dramatize. Shout when a character shouts. Jump when a character is afraid.

6. Read and record

If you come across a good story as you read, clip it, copy it, or write it down and file it away. Create an electronic file of stories you can refer to when you're preparing a message. Give your stories subject headings so you can find them using your computer's search function. Be sure to give credit to the source for any stories you use.

CROSS REFERENCE:
For other sermon- and illustration-organization suggestions, see "3 Ways to Organize Your Used Sermons and Illustrations," in Section 2, page 48.

7. Resurrect old sources

Visit used bookstores and check out sections that contain books of illustrations for speaking. At garage sales, used bookstores, and special library sales, look for old issues of Reader's Digest—these are full of forgotten stories that can find new life in your sermons. People might know stories from recent books and magazines, but they probably won't recognize great stories from older sources.

8. Mine your own experiences

Many pastors effectively tell stories from their own lives. Of course, if you overdo that, people will get bored. But you can tell the same stories anonymously. Grab "anything and everything" that happens to you and use these events as stories for sermons. Personal stories often have a humorous punch line, so they do double duty—providing inspiration and giving people a laugh as well.

9. Use stories from your church and community

Cultivate staff members and/or key people from your congregation who know a good story when they hear it. As they come across good stories in their reading, in the life of the church, and in their communities, they can e-mail the stories to you. This is more than just a good way to get stories. It also involves key people in your preaching.

10. Read children's books

Children's books often focus on simple lessons of right and wrong. You can retell part of a children's story in your sermon, or—because these books are so brief—you might be able to read a whole story to your congregation. Head to your local library and ask the children's librarian for picture books that are short (less than 500 words). Review the library's copies and buy your own from a local or online bookstore to keep in your own library.

11. Tell great stories of our culture

Classic novels such as *To Kill a Mockingbird, Moby-Dick,* and *The Scarlet Letter* all provide great grist for the preacher's mill. Some of your listeners will be familiar with these stories, but many won't. The ones who do know the stories will be impressed with your knowledge and breadth of learning and will listen to your messages with additional interest, knowing that you'll spice up sermons with great stories and anecdotes.

12. Tell stories of hymns, songs, and other pieces of music

You'll discover tremendous stories about the writing of many hymns and praise choruses on the Internet. Search for terms such as "Stories Behind Christian Hymns." A number of books tell stories of great hymns, such as *Great Christian Hymn Writers* by Jane Stuart Smith and Betty Carlson (Crossway Books, 1997) and *101 Hymn Stories* by Kenneth W. Osbeck (Kregel, 1982).

10 Ready-to-Use Movie Illustrations

Movie clips make great sermon illustrations. The following clips are ready to plug into your sermons. Use the questions to help you write your message, or drive the lesson home by asking people to discuss a question with the person next to them for a minute or two.

1. *National Treasure* (PG)

Topic: Finding the treasure of salvation
Clip Location: The very beginning of the movie; DVD chapter 1
Story Context: A great treasure has been hidden for centuries, with clues left for those who might seek it.
Start Cue: A boy goes into the attic with a flashlight.
Stop Cue: The grandfather unfolds a dollar bill and says, "They're speaking to us through these."
Scripture Links: Deuteronomy 4:29; Jeremiah 29:12-13; Matthew 7:7-8
Questions:
- In what ways is the path to salvation like following a treasure map?
- How easy or hard is it for you to follow the "clues" in the Bible that lead to the treasure of eternal life?
- How would you describe the treasure that God has for you?
- Have you shared your "treasure" with other people or have you kept it to yourself? What can you do to be able to share your treasure more freely?

2. *The Tigger Movie* (G)

Topic: Are people or work more important?
Clip Location: 47 minutes into the movie; DVD chapter 16
Story Context: Tigger's friends are planning a family reunion for him because he's missing his family. They want to show him that they, his friends, are his family. But Rabbit insists there's no time for fun—there's too much work to do.
Start Cue: Owl says, "A veritable work of art."
Stop Cue: Rabbit slams the door shut.
Scripture Link: Luke 10:38-42
Questions:
- Tigger's friends were most concerned about doing something for their friend, but Rabbit was most concerned about making important preparations for winter. Which do you think is most important, and why?

- Read Luke 10:38-42. What does Jesus say is most important?
- If the Bible says it's important for us to do our best work, why did Jesus say that Mary did the important thing?

3. *Dave* (PG-13)

Topic: Feeling inadequate for God's call on your life
Clip Location: 19 minutes into the movie; DVD chapter 7
Story Context: Dave is asked to stand in for the president, who is in a coma.
Start Cue: "I'm Alan Reed."
Stop Cue: Dave sits down on the couch.
Scripture Links: Exodus 4:10-17; Matthew 10:18-20
Questions:

- Dave felt like he was being asked to do something that was out of his league. Have you ever felt that way about something God asked you to do?
- Have you ever asked God to find someone else for a task like Dave did?
- Why does God ask us to do things that feel impossible to us?

4. *The Santa Clause 2* (G)

Topic: Belief/faith
Clip Location: 54 minutes into the movie; DVD chapter 11
Story Context: Scott Calvin is actually Santa Claus. He's taking a sleigh ride with Carol, and they're discussing Christmas.
Start Cue: "When did you become such a cynic?"
Stop Cue: "Yes, I know."
Scripture Links: Hebrews 11; 1 Peter 1:6-12
Questions:

- Do you believe these things exist, even if you haven't seen them: a million dollars; another solar system; wind; atoms? Why?
- Why do kids believe in Santa Claus even if they haven't seen him?
- How is believing in God like or unlike a child's believing in Santa Claus?
- Why does God ask us to believe in him based on faith rather than proof?

5. *A Christmas Story* (PG)

Topic: Learning to tame the tongue
Clip Location: 18 minutes into the movie; DVD chapter 7
Story Context: Kids on a playground dare a boy to lick a flagpole in the middle of winter.
Start Cue: A kid says, "Go on and do it." *(Note: There's swearing in this line of dialogue, so be sure to start the clip right after it's said.)*
Stop Cue: A teacher in a classroom
Scripture Links: Psalm 15:1-3; Proverbs 11:8-12; James 3:1-12
Questions:

- When has your tongue gotten you in trouble?
- Why is it so hard to control our tongues?
- What does Scripture say about the damage we can do to others with our words?
- How can we learn to control what comes out of our mouths?

6. *Serendipity* (PG-13)

Topic: God's plan for our lives; free will
Clip Location: About 5 minutes into the movie; DVD chapter 1
Story Context: Jonathan and Sara discuss the role of fate in their lives.
Start Cue: "This is the ultimate blended drink."
Stop Cue: "You have a boyfriend, right?"
Scripture Links: Joshua 24:15; Isaiah 55:6-9; Jeremiah 29:11-13
Questions:

- Do you believe something greater than ourselves controls what happens in our lives? Do you think that "something greater" is fate? destiny? chance? God?
- Does God give us free will to make our own decisions or does he control everything? Why do you believe that?

7. *Finding Nemo* (G)

Topic: Temptation
Clip Location: 32 minutes into the movie; DVD chapter 11
Story Context: Two fish see a beautiful light in the ocean and decide to follow it, but it turns out to be a dangerous fish that tries to eat them.
Start Cue: "Dory, do you see anything?"
Stop Cue: "The mask!"
Scripture Links: Matthew 26:36-46; 1 Corinthians 10:12-13; 1 Timothy 6:6-10; James 1:13-15

Questions:

- Have you ever encountered something that looked good on the surface but was really an invitation to sin? What did you *want* to do? What did you *actually* do?
- Why does sin seem so inviting?
- How can we tell between sin and something that's actually good?

8. *I, Robot* (PG-13)

Topic: We were created for a purpose.
Clip Location: 1 hour, 8 minutes into the movie; DVD chapter 24
Story Context: A robot describes his dream of someone coming to save us, and he says he believes we were all created for a purpose.
Start Cue: Two people walk into a room with a robot. "Authorized entry."
Stop Cue: "We all have a purpose. Don't you think, Detective?"
Scripture Links: Psalm 138; Romans 8:28-29; 9:17
Questions:

- Do you think we each have a purpose? What do you think your purpose is?
- Do you believe that God also created each of us for a specific purpose? How can we discover what that purpose is?

9. *Monsters, Inc.* (G)

Topic: Fear
Clip Location: 44 minutes into the movie; DVD chapter 23
Story Context: Sully is a monster who has befriended a little girl he calls Boo. But Sully's boss makes him scare another child, and Boo sees his "monstrous" side.
Start Cue: "No, no, no, no, no."
Stop Cue: "The child!"
Scripture Links: Isaiah 41:10-13; Romans 8:15-17; 1 John 4:16-18
Questions:

- What makes you afraid? Why?
- How do you respond when you're confronted with something you fear?
- Why don't we have to be afraid?
- How does God help us with our fears?

10. *The Incredibles* (PG)

Topic: Making family a priority

Clip Location: 1 hour, 30 minutes into the movie; DVD chapter 25

Story Context: A family of superheroes is trapped by their nemesis, and the father realizes he's been missing out on family life.

Start Cue: "I'm sorry. This is my fault."

Stop Cue: "I think it's time to wind down now."

Scripture Links: Ephesians 5:22-33; 1 Timothy 3:2-5; 1 Peter 3:1-7

Questions:

- Where is your family among your life's priorities?
- Do your actions toward them and the time you spend with them reflect that priority?
- What things bind you and keep you from your family?
- What bonds do you need to break to make your family the priority they should be in your life?

4 Web Sites for Movie Clip Illustrations

In addition to the ready-to-use clips listed above, check the following Web sites for similar clips that you can use as sermon illustrations. (Note: It may be necessary to subscribe to these sites to access certain content.)

1. www.ministryandmedia.com

While this site is geared toward youth pastors, you'll find plenty of movie illustrations to use for your sermons. The site is regularly updated with Scriptures and discussion questions linked to newly released films, along with a database of movies on DVD and video.

2. www.screenvue.com

Join this site to find movie clips you can show under a CVLI license (see the "Movie Copyrights" sidebar). You can also get DVDs and CD-ROMs with pre-edited clips from Christian and independent film producers.

3. www.movieministry.com

This site lists hundreds of sermon illustrations from movie clips. It also offers a searchable database, plus newsletters about Christianity and media.

4. www.textweek.com/movies/themeindex.htm

Here you'll find a long list of movie themes you can use for sermon illustrations.

MOVIE COPYRIGHTS

Movies are copyrighted material, and copyright laws apply to showing clips from them. Christian Video Licensing International is an organization that can help you stay legal when using movie clips. It's related to CCLI, a licensing organization for the songs and hymns you reprint or project on screen.

According to www.cvli.org, "Churches and other ministry organizations can show videos and be in accordance with the U.S. Copyright Act by using one of the following methods:

1. Showing videos which have 'Public Performance Rights,'
2. Receiving written permission prior to using the video, or
3. Obtaining coverage with the Church Video License."

10 Interactive and Memorable Object Lessons

Mustard seeds, fish, coins, lilies, building stones, and sparrows—Jesus understood the power of using everyday objects to powerfully communicate spiritual truth. You can follow his example by using simple objects in your sermons. Use the following ideas to create poignant, memorable, and meaningful object lessons that will help your congregation understand scriptural truths and apply them to life.

1. Getting Past the Past

Objects: Full-length mirror, dry-erase marker, cloth
Suggested Scriptures: Psalms 32:1-5; 103:8-14; 1 Corinthians 6:9-11
Illustration: By writing sins on a mirror and then looking at your reflection, you can illustrate for worshippers how we often allow sins from the past to color and distort our view of ourselves today.
The Object Lesson:

Set up the mirror so that it faces the congregation. As you begin your sermon, tell stories of sins and wrong things you did as a child. Each time you name a sin, write it on the mirror in big block letters. Continue by naming sins you committed as a teenager and as an adult, each time writing the sin boldly on the mirror. Once the mirror is mostly covered, say: **Many of you probably have a list very similar to mine. And these are just the sins I feel comfortable telling you about. Most people hide many sins that they are too ashamed to mention.**

Name additional sins that people might hide—like lust, adultery, pornography, abuse—and write each on the mirror.

Then stand in front of the mirror and look at yourself so that the congregation can see your reflection, covered with the words written on the mirror. Smile at yourself in the mirror.

Say: **This is how many of us live our lives. We smile for the outside world and act like we're fine. But sins from our past haunt us, warp our relationships, and distort our perspective of ourselves.**

Use this activity to launch into a sermon about God's grace and forgiveness. Later in the sermon, use a piece of cloth to erase the words, then stand in front of the mirror to exemplify the true forgiveness and power to change that we find in Christ.

2. God's Plan for Sexuality

Objects: Goldfish in a fishbowl, fishnet

Suggested Scriptures: Song of Solomon; 1 Corinthians 6:18-20; Hebrews 13:4

Illustration: Just as God created fish to live and thrive in an aquatic environment, he created sexual activity to be enjoyed within the bounds of marriage.

The Object Lesson:

As you explain that God created sex solely to be enjoyed within the confines of marriage, take out the fishbowl and set it on the podium. Explain that God created fish to thrive in one environment—water. Use the fishnet to scoop a goldfish out of the water. Momentarily hold it out of the water and say: **This is still a goldfish, but it's no longer in the environment God created it for. It's still alive, but if I keep it out of the water much longer, the fish will die.** Church members will definitely get the point when you (temporarily) remove a goldfish from its bowl!

Wait a few seconds longer, then put the fish back in the water. Explain that when we take sex out of the environment God created it for, it ceases to be what God intended it to be. Sure, it can still be pleasurable, but it's robbed of the bonding, trusting, and loving intimacy God made it to be. Instead of being a beautiful celebration of married love, it hurts and damages the lives of those involved.

3. God's Purpose for Friendship

Objects: Inflatable balloons, flannel sheet

Suggested Scriptures: Psalm 1; Proverbs 17:17; 27:5-6, 9-10, 17; Ecclesiastes 4:9-10; 1 Thessalonians 5:11

Illustration: A balloon generates static electricity when rubbed on a person's hair or certain fabrics. This provides a picture of God's purpose for friendship: When we spend time with friends of good character, their good example rubs off on us and helps us to do things we can't do on our own!

The Object Lesson:

Invite a few volunteers to come up to the front and join you in inflating some balloons. You'll want one or two balloons per person. (You can also have balloons already inflated before the sermon.) Ask the volunteers to rub their balloons on themselves (their clothes or hair) or on a flannel sheet attached to the wall in order to create static. When a volunteer thinks his balloon is good and staticky, he should try to stick it to the wall. Volunteers can also try to use static to affix their balloons to each other's backs. Once the team of volunteers has made several of the balloons stick, thank them for their help and lead the congregation in applauding them as they return to their seats.

Use the activity to make the point that just as the static electricity caused by rubbing the balloons on fabric caused them to "stick," similarly something special happens when we're in close contact with Christian friends. Good character rubs off! Use this point to kick off a sermon on the qualities of Christian friendship, the importance of accountability, and the contagiousness of good character.

4. The Holy Spirit at Work Within Us

Objects: A batch of unleavened bread dough, a batch of leavened
      bread dough, two warmed glass bowls, two damp cloths
Suggested Scriptures: John 16:7-15; Ephesians 3:14-21
Illustration: Yeast causes bread dough to rise and grow; without yeast,
      no amount of kneading and stretching will cause dough to rise.
      Like yeast worked into dough, the Holy Spirit works within us to
      grow us and change us in ways we can't accomplish on our own.
The Object Lesson:

Before the sermon, recruit a baker (a homemaker or professional) from your congregation to help you by preparing two batches of bread dough. One batch should be unleavened dough. The other leavened batch should be prepared the morning of the worship service. Tell the baker you want the dough to already be rising at the start of the service.

At the start of the worship service, have the baker help you in the front of the sanctuary by placing the unleavened dough in a glass bowl and covering it with a cloth, then placing the rising dough in a warmed glass bowl and covering that with another cloth. Be sure that the congregation is able to see what you're doing.

During your sermon, after the correct amount of time has elapsed, take the cloth off of the first glass bowl and reveal the unleavened dough. Squeeze it, stretch it, and pound it, then say: **No amount of kneading will cause this dough to rise. It's missing yeast, the critical ingredient to make it rise.**

Then take the cloth off the second bowl and reveal the leavened dough, which should have doubled in size. Say: **The yeast in this dough is changing it—literally altering its chemical makeup. It's growing and rising in ways this other batch of dough never will. The change in the dough isn't due to any effort of the dough's—it can't will itself to rise. It's all due to the yeast at work inside.**

Then continue, by saying: **Like the yeast in the dough, we have the Holy Spirit at work within us. The Holy Spirit empowers us to change, causes us to grow, and enables us to become who God created us to be.**

Continue with your sermon explaining the presence and work of the Holy Spirit in the life of Christians.

Bonus Idea: At the end of the worship service, if possible, distribute slices of freshly baked bread for church members to eat as a celebration of what they learned about the work of the Holy Spirit in their lives.

5. In Your Light We See Light

Objects: A glow-in-the-dark toy in a paper bag, desk lamp, and a very large cardboard box

Suggested Scriptures: Psalm 36:3-9; Matthew 5:14-16; John 15:1-5; 1 John 1:5-7

Illustration: A glow-in-the-dark object only glows after it has been near a bright light source. Similarly, as we spend time drawing closer to God, we begin to "glow," shining the light of God's love for those around us to see.

The Object Lesson:

Invite an elementary-aged child to help you with this illustration. Ask the child to come up to the front. Say: **I've got something really special to show you!**

Prompt the child to reach into the paper bag and take out the glow-in-the-dark toy. Say: **This toy can do something really cool!** Invite your volunteer to sit on the floor and hold the glow-in-the-dark toy, and then set the cardboard box on top of the child so that he or she is momentarily in the dark. Ask:

- **Can you see anything? Is it doing anything special?** The answer should be no. Because the toy was in the bag, it wasn't exposed to the light necessary to cause it to glow.

Lift the box off of the child. Say: **I know something we can try! If you hold the toy right next to this bright light for a few minutes, I think we'll be able to make it glow. Can you help me?**

Turn on the desk lamp and instruct the child to hold the toy right next to the light source for a few minutes. (Note: You'll want to test beforehand to see how long it will take the toy to begin glowing.) During this time, read the Scripture you've selected for your sermon. When you're done reading the verses, ask the child to sit on the floor again, holding the toy. Place the cardboard box over the child so he or she's in the dark. Ask the child to shout out what he or she observes about the glow toy. This time it should clearly glow in the dark. Afterward, thank the child and have the congregation applaud as the child returns to his or her seat.

Use this example as a powerful visual image of the importance of being close to God and abiding in him. The more we spend time with him, the better we reflect his light in a dark world.

Bonus Idea: Give each worshipper a glow-in-the-dark star to take home. Explain to the congregation that the star can remind them of their desire to abide close to Christ and to glow with *his* light!

6. Money Doesn't Satisfy

Objects: Several caffeinated drinks

Suggested Scriptures: Ecclesiastes (especially 5:8-20); Matthew 6:19-24; 1 Timothy 6:6-10; Hebrews 13:5-6

Illustration: Although caffeinated drinks are popular thirst-quenchers, the caffeine in them actually causes *dehydration*. Of course, this is the opposite effect we want from a beverage. Just as these drinks do not deliver the desired effect, people often accumulate money and objects as a way to satisfy their spiritual needs. In the end, though, they're left feeling empty and unsatisfied.

The Object Lesson:

Begin your sermon by inviting some volunteers to come to the front. Give them each a caffeinated drink such as a frozen blended coffee drink or an ice-cold can of cola.

Ask the volunteers:

• How are your drinks? Are they refreshing?

Let the volunteers return to their seats (with their drinks), and then make the point that the drinks represent a sad truth about our society. Explain that although people often enjoy those types of drinks as a source of refreshment, the caffeine actually makes them *thirstier.* Similarly, people try to fill their lives with "stuff" in order to feel satisfied, but end up feeling greater emptiness and less fulfillment as a result of their materialism.

7. Sin—We All Fall Short

Objects: Cotton balls

Suggested Scripture: Romans 3:19-24

Illustration: A chasm of sin separates imperfect humans from our perfect and holy God. No matter how hard we try, we can't cross the chasm by our own good works. Volunteers will illustrate this point by attempting to throw cotton balls across the width of the sanctuary.

The Object Lesson:

Before the sermon, arrange for several volunteers of various ages and athletic abilities to help you with this activity. If possible, try to include at least one elementary-school aged child, two teenagers (a guy and a girl), several adults of various ages, and at least one senior adult.

Begin by inviting the volunteers to stand next to you. Give each a cotton ball and announce to the congregation that the volunteers will now demonstrate how to throw a cotton ball all the way across the room. Let each volunteer try to toss a cotton ball as far as possible. No one will be able to throw one very far! Make sure the volunteers don't doctor their cotton balls by squishing them, wetting them, or by any other method to increase their "throwability."

When all have tried, say: **Well, none of you got it across the room, but thanks for trying!** Lead the congregation in applauding the volunteers, then transition into your sermon.

Use this activity to illustrate the meaning of Romans 3:23. While some of the volunteers were able to throw their cotton balls farther than others, *no one* was able to even get *close* to the other side of the room. Similarly, while some people live better lives than others—giving to charity, volunteering, saying positive things—none of us even comes close to God's perfection. An Olympic gold-medal shot-putter would still not be able to toss a cotton ball across the room; similarly, a model citizen and highly moral person cannot come close to God's holiness and perfection. We *all* sin and we *all* fall short of God's glory. We all need God's gift of salvation.

8. Suffering

Objects: Manure, small spade or shovel, small flowering plant without its pot, garden pot, gardening gloves, plastic sheet

Suggested Scriptures: Romans 5:3-5; 8:16-28; Philippians 3:7-11; 1 Peter 4:12-19

Illustration: Sometimes life stinks! Suffering and hardship can make us feel like we're stuck in a pile of…well…manure. But just as manure is a natural fertilizer filled with nutrients that help plants grow, suffering can be the right spiritual environment for God to help us grow in new and amazing ways.

The Object Lesson:

Before the sermon, cover part of the floor with a plastic sheet and place a medium-sized pile of manure on top. Manure is available at stores that sell gardening supplies. Set a small plant and a small spade or shovel near the manure. Keep the gardening gloves hidden.

Invite two or three junior-high students to come to the front, and tell them that you need their help planting something. When they seem ready, say: **OK, I'll need you to put the plant in this pot, and then grab some manure and pat it around the plant really good with your bare hands. Sound good? By the way, do you know what manure is?**

Allow them to share their answers, then explain (in appropriate language, of course) what manure is. Invite the kids to bend down and give it a sniff (but if they pass on the offer, that's OK!).

After the kids have expressed some hesitation to touch the manure, thank them for their efforts and let them take their seats, inviting the congregation to applaud them for their "help." If some kids *are* willing to help you put the plant in the manure, let them and encourage them to use the bathroom afterward to wash their hands. Better yet, keep some paper towels or moist wipes up front, just in case.

Use this activity to make the point that sometimes life can seem like a big pile of manure! Unpleasantness, hassle, pain, persecution, illness, financial hardship, disaster—these and many other causes of emotional pain and spiritual suffering can plague us and make our lives *stink*. We tend to avoid suffering at all costs.

If the plant hasn't been put into the pot yet, take out your gardening gloves now and plant it, and explain that manure is actually full of nutrients and minerals that work as a natural fertilizer. Gardeners and farmers use manure all the time to help their plants and vegetables grow and thrive. Discuss the passage you've chosen, and explain that sometimes God plants us in the midst of suffering and unpleasantness. God can use the pain and hard times in our lives to help us grow and develop in ways we never would have otherwise.

9. Taming the Tongue

Objects: Several pieces of chewing gum, garbage can
Suggested Scriptures: Ephesians 4:29-32; Colossians 3:8-10;
James 1:19-26; 3:3-12
Illustration: It's tough to understand what someone is trying to say when his mouth is full of chewing gum! Similarly, when a Christian has habits of using unkind words, the message of the gospel he or she may be trying to communicate becomes garbled and distorted.

The Object Lesson:
At the beginning of your sermon, put a piece of chewing gum in your mouth and chew it noticeably while you begin speaking. About a minute later, unwrap another piece of gum and put it in your mouth. Continue chewing while you keep talking. Keep adding pieces until you've got a large wad of gum in your mouth. Of course, at this point it will be virtually impossible for the congregation to understand what you're saying. For a few moments, pretend that there isn't a problem, and then remove the gum.

Use this illustration to make the point that unkind words—like gossip, slander, cursing, or angry words—hinder the message of the gospel. We can't adequately communicate the love of Christ to others when our habits cause us to speak in ways that don't honor God. Our message becomes garbled, distorted, and blocked by our un-Christlike habits of speaking.

10. Uniquely Gifted for God's Good Purpose

Objects: Several odd or unique kitchen gadgets, such as an egg separator, a garlic press, a pastry mixer, a flour sifter, a meat thermometer, a zester, a salad spinner, a lemon press, and a tea infuser

Suggested Scriptures: 1 Corinthians 1:4-9; 12:1-11; Ephesians 4:7-16; Philippians 2:12-13

Illustration: Each kitchen gadget has a unique purpose. Each is perfectly suited for the task it was created to accomplish. Similarly, God gives all Christians talents and spiritual gifts that equip us to accomplish God's purposes for us.

The Object Lesson:

Invite several young children to help you start your sermon. Give each child a unique or odd kitchen gadget, then say: **Each of these objects has a very special purpose—something unique it can do to accomplish a specific job.** Ask: **What do you think your object does?**

Encourage kids to take creative guesses at what their objects are or what they do. Affirm the children's guesses, then lead the congregation in applauding them while they take their seats.

Hold up each item and share with the congregation (especially for the culinarily-challenged) what each one is and what it does. Then say: **You, too, were created for a purpose. You are uniquely made and distinctively gifted for specific ways God wants to use you. Don't believe me? Let's look at what the Bible says.**

Continue with your sermon by examining spiritual gifts and passages about God's purposes for each Christian.

8 Ways to Incorporate the Arts Into Your Sermons

Many pastors today are finding that all kinds of arts provide ways to illustrate sermons. How can you learn to incorporate the arts into your sermons? Consider the following ideas.

1. Drama: Skits

A skit performed by several actors can provide a great comedic or dramatic punch to your sermon. Many skits for use in sermons are available online, including:

- Lillenas: www.lillenasdrama.com
- Meriwether: www.meriwetherpublishing.com
- Eldridge Christian Plays: www.95church.com
- Willow Creek Association: www.willowcreek.com

Stopping in the middle of your sermon for a drama team to perform a skit can nail home a point. People will still remember the skit and the point it was illustrating long after they've forgotten the rest of the sermon.

2. Drama: Plays

This longer type of drama can be more difficult to incorporate into a single sermon, but a play can follow your sermon or vice-versa. The play might include a worshipful or outreach-focused message that you then emphasize with a follow-up sermon. Or a longer play could replace the sermon. God will use your creative efforts if you're willing to think outside the box.

3. Dance

Liturgical dance has a strong presence in many churches. Chances are, your church has one or more members with an interest in dance, including ballet, jazz dance, and contemporary dance. You might include dance in your sermons in several ways: a solo dancer on stage, dance supported by a narrator, or dance with accompanying music. With a solid introduction and some words about the dance's meaning, most congregations can enjoy an artist honestly portraying an element of worship through dance.

4. Poetry

While modern poetry can be difficult to understand and even inaccessible, some poetry coming out of the church carries powerful meaning and can strengthen a sagging sermon. Modern Christian poets like Luci Shaw and Calvin Miller provide material that is both potent and touching. The accessible and easy-to-understand contemporary poetry of individuals such as Anne Sexton, Ted Hughes, Sylvia Plath, Charles Simic, Mark Strand, and others contain compelling messages that you can weave into your sermon's fabric. In addition, favorite poets of years gone by— Gerard Manley Hopkins, Elizabeth Barrett Browning, Robert Frost, William Shakespeare, John Donne, and John Milton—have startlingly unique and potent poems that can illustrate part of a sermon. Find a church member with a good voice who knows how to read poetry dramatically.

5. Responsive readings

Two to five actors perform these readings on stage while sitting on tall stools. Sometimes called "reader's theatre," these readings can include plays (not acted out, but read) or responsive readings. Often they incorporate Scripture with narration. An online search for "church responsive readings" will produce many usable results.

6. Paintings and other color media

While these art techniques can be a bit more difficult to bring into sermons, you can use video or photography to display them on a large screen. For years, pastors have used "chalk talks" to great effect. Even if you can't draw, you can have an artist draw or paint a picture illustrating the sermon's theme.

BANNER NOTE:

Other banner ideas can be found in "8 Ways to Revitalize Your Worship Space," Section 3, page 73.

Some churches use colorful banners in their sanctuaries. You can ask a fabric artist to create banners that accentuate your message or to craft banners that add general beauty and communicate truth into the worship space.

7. Clay and sculpture

Get your congregation involved in your sermon by providing small pieces of clay or Play-Doh and having each person sculpt something in response to part of your message. For example, they could sculpt something to finish the statement, "I love…" or, "Something I need to pray about is…"

8. Music

Music falls into the category of arts, and you can experiment with incorporating music into your sermons. Ask a group of musicians to perform a thoughtful contemporary piece of rock, blues, jazz, or country while you weave the words of the song into your message.

You could also preach a series of sermons on contemporary issues found in the latest rap, pop, or rock music. Use the message of a song by playing a portion to your congregation, and then tie it in to points from Scripture. Start by exploring the subjects in songs like "Adam's Song" by Blink-182, "Father of Mine" and "Wonderful" by Everclear, and "Crumbs at Your Table" and "Sunday Bloody Sunday" by U2.

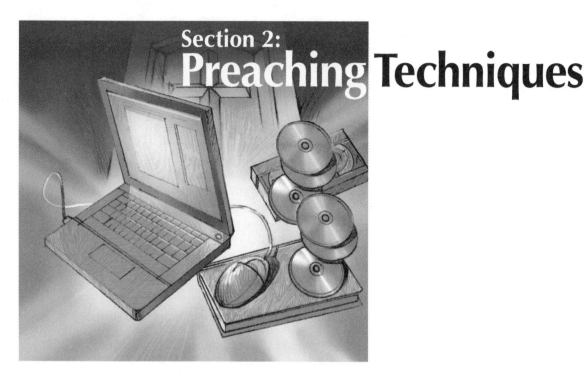

Section 2:
Preaching Techniques

You've come up with some creative content for your sermons, but what about the technical aspects of preaching? "Technical" in this sense carries a broad meaning—covering everything from technology to speaking techniques to getting organized. Think of the nuts and bolts or the mechanics of preparing and delivering your messages. Of course, you're going to rely on God to speak through you as you preach. But he also wants you to be prepared. The ideas in this section will help you get ready to preach in both basic and surprising ways.

Section 2: Table of Contents

21 Creative Ways to Use Media and Technology in Sermons

What would you do without technology? Computers, software, projection equipment, the Internet, and many other electronic tools have changed the way nearly all pastors approach their ministries. The following ideas offer ways you can use technology before, during, and after you develop your sermons.

Before the Sermon

1. Search the Internet

Use search engines such as Google (www.google.com) or Yahoo (www.yahoo.com) to search for photos and drawings to use in your message. Be sure the search filter is turned on (look for "Preferences" and set to "safe search")—even innocent-sounding searches can return some pretty rotten photos. Once you've found a photo you like, use simple photo manipulation software to crop the picture to best suit your needs.

Remember also that Web sites are protected by copyright laws, so be sure you obtain permission for any materials you use. Look for a "Terms and Conditions" link at the bottom of the Web page you're referencing. (If still in doubt, click the "Contact us" link, and *ask*.)

2. Keep it stylish, but simple

Keep up to date with electronic publishing styles by observing well-designed Internet sites. Styles continue to change. PowerPoint novices usually use too many fonts and bad color combinations. When in doubt, keep it as simple as possible.

3. Practice for disaster

The individuals who run PowerPoint and related hardware and software should be prepared for what to do if something goes wrong. At the very least, they should know who can help immediately. What does the PowerPoint operator do if the screen goes blank or the laptop shuts off? Write out steps to take when different situations occur. Similarly, you should be prepared to carry on with your sermon even if the problems can't be resolved.

4. Read your slides—
before your congregation does

Set up a system of editing or review for any text that you project. This will save you from an embarrassing error on the screen while you're teaching. Make sure that more than one set of eyes reviews each slide.

5. Make sure your slides are readable

Being able to read projected text is most important. What you see on the computer screen is not necessarily how text and images will look when projected. Test it. Stand in the back of your auditorium and see how each slide looks with various lighting conditions.

6. Don't overload your slides

When a PowerPoint slide contains too much information, your congregation faces the choice of listening to your message and trying to comprehend the slide at the same time. Be sure that the slide supports what you're saying. One guideline to follow is for a slide to contain no more than what you'd want listeners to write down if they're taking notes. Of course, you'll make exceptions, such as when you want to display a quote or a Scripture passage.

For Studying

7. Books on CD

By collecting books on CD—including many titles now in public domain—you can carry a whole library in your briefcase. At first, you might feel uncomfortable reading books on a computer screen, but with time it will become natural. You can also load books into your personal digital assistant (PDA) to read almost anywhere during idle time.

8. Study online

Study on the Internet. Many pastors and teachers make their notes and sermon outlines available so that you can find them with a quick search. Much of this material is free and can help you jump-start your own study. (Just remember to credit your source if you incorporate their ideas—see also Tip 1 on page 42.)

9. Back up your work

Don't spend hours studying and then lose it due to a power loss or computer crash. Back up your work and keep the backup in a safe place. How often should you back up? As often as you wouldn't want to redo what you have already done. You can't control power surges, viruses, software problems, and hardware failures. Always be prepared with copies of your work.

10. Get training

Ask around your congregation to find the most tech-savvy teenager in your church. Pay that individual twice the minimum wage to show you how to use your computer and software. It's better than a class and tailored exactly to your needs.

During the Sermon

11. Use PowerPoint to show your key points

PowerPoint slides add a visual dimension to your sermon and also help people in your congregation take notes by identifying your outline, key points, and Scripture references. If the words appear on the screen, the congregation knows they're important.

12. Use illustrations

A single photo, illustration, or graphic can clarify a difficult concept (spiritual armor, the tabernacle, temple furniture), or add emphasis to a truth (father holding his son, sunrise, barren desert). Project a map to help explain ancient locations, or show a graphic to help explain the meaning of a Greek word.

RECOMMENDED RESOURCE:

News You Can Use: 101 Sermon Illustrations by Mikal Keefer (Group)—includes a CD-ROM with more than 200 ready-to-go PowerPoint slides.

13. Break down the steps

Take a single PowerPoint slide and create multiple slides. Show the steps by manually forwarding the slides or have them automatically proceed as you talk. For example, when teaching on the fruits of the Spirit, show an illustration of a tree. As you proceed to the next "fruit," click forward and the new word appears in the tree.

During a summary at the end of your message, the words could appear in order after time delays as you are speaking.

14. Focus on Scripture

Don't make projecting Scripture on the screen a substitute for the Bible. However, if you need to work through a number of different passages quickly, displaying the reference and passage helps keep people focused on the point you're making rather than trying to find the last two verses you read.

15. Congregational Scripture reading

People come to church with different Bible translations. Others might not have a Bible. Yet others might be completely unfamiliar with Scripture. By projecting a passage, the entire congregation can read it aloud together.

16. Highlight your key words

When you use PowerPoint to highlight a key word or phrase in a passage, people learn to see it in context.

For Other Parts of the Service

17. Announcements

Use PowerPoint software to cycle through announcements before your services or other events, incorporating eye-catching graphics. This is a good time to experiment and have fun with the clever animated features of the technology. Some ideas:

- Upcoming events. Photos and graphics add to the excitement of an upcoming event. Showing photos of people having fun at previous events brings back fun memories and creates anticipation. Humor goes a long way—photos from last year's junior high all-night lock-in should make people laugh. However, remember that some events obviously deserve a more serious treatment.
- Birthdays and anniversaries. Project a list of the current week's birthdays and anniversaries to remind your congregation that you're all a family. Photos also work well—show both the wedding photo and a current photo of a couple celebrating their 50th anniversary.
- Feature a missionary. Encourage prayer for missionaries by projecting a missionary family's photo, key facts, and recent prayer requests.

CROSS REFERENCE:
Also see "14 Creative Ways to Support Missionaries," Section 8, page 217.

- Feature a ministry. Showing photos and fast facts about a ministry within the church reminds people of the importance of prayer, giving, and serving to keep each ministry going.

18. Worship preparation

Show worship music videos before a church service or event. Available on DVD, these videos combine uplifting music and quality video ranging from edgy urban scenes to majestic landscapes. Several Christian music publishers produce these products, so you can probably find a video that meets your specific need or theme. Check out some samples by clicking on the DVD button at www.worshipmusic.com.

19. Singing

When it comes to creating the music portion of your worship service, you're no longer bound to singing songs only in the way they're printed. Because people no longer need to turn pages, you can arrange psalms, hymns, and spiritual songs in any order.

Include congregational readings between songs. For singing or reading, mark the PowerPoint slide with cues to give your congregation a creative part in the worship service—the words "solo" or "leader" can inform the congregation to be quiet during part of the song or reading. When implementing this, start simply—but don't ever let it get too complicated.

20. Instrumental music

Display the words to a song during an instrument-only performance (such as a prelude, offering time, or postlude). Many instrumentalists will appreciate that attention is being drawn away from their skill so that the music instead emphasizes the message of the song.

For the Future

21. Think long term

Save your sermon outlines, commentaries, and ideas in a popular word-processing program such as Word or WordPerfect. Each time a computer operating system advances, some software packages become obsolete. Trying to retrieve information you've saved in an old and obsolete program can be extremely difficult.

Also, be careful of imbedding sermon notes in presentation software. PowerPoint, for example, allows you to attach notes to a presentation. However, when you need to teach the material without using PowerPoint, your work can be difficult to extract and use in another teaching environment. Similarly, some Bible study programs also offer ways to attach notes to specific texts, but if the program becomes obsolete, you might not be able to extract the material you've imbedded in it.

Keeping your hard work in an easily accessible format can save you from future heartache. (Also see "3 Ways to Organize Your Used Sermons and Illustrations," on the following page.)

3 Ways to Organize Your Used Sermons and Illustrations

Take a look at a typical pastor's desk, and you're likely to find piles of clippings, periodicals, illustrations, books, tapes, seminar notes, and other gems. Most pastors realize that organizing their sermons and illustrations can save countless hours of frustration. The following ideas can help you accurately track your preaching and teaching material.

1. Electronic storage

Store each sermon as an electronic folder of notes, outlines, illustrations, and other elements. Think of your computer's hard drive as a massive electronic filing cabinet, and set up folders and individual files to put in its drawers. Specifically, try the following suggestions:

- Create two primary folders—one for sermons and one for illustrations.
- Within the sermons folder, create a subfolder for each book of the Bible and a subfolder for any theme or topic you preach on, and file your sermons in the appropriate folder. If your sermon includes a primary portion of Scripture and also follows a strong theme, store a copy in each folder.
- Create the file name for each sermon document with a portion of the sermon title and the date when you preached it for quick and easy reference. For example, you might name a file for the sermon "God's Grace in Tough Times" that you preached on September 9, 2006, as GodsGrace090906.
- Within the illustrations folder, create subfolders for various illustration topics such as anger, aging, humor, grief, and so forth. As you collect or use illustrations, create an electronic document for each one and file it in the appropriate topical folder. Create a file name for each document, using the first few words of the quote or illustration for easy reference. For example, you might use the file name AmazingGrace.HymnStories for an illustration that tells the story behind the hymn "Amazing Grace."

Experiment with and adapt your filing system and file names until you have what works best for you.

Also, don't forget to back up your folders and files regularly (perhaps weekly or monthly). If you use writeable CDs to back up your files, create two copies—one set for your office at church and another set for home. Another backup option involves opening a Gmail account. Gmail (http://mail.google.com) is a search-based Web mail service that currently offers more than two gigabytes of free storage, a built-in Google search that instantly finds any message you want, automatic arrangement of messages and related replies into "conversations," and text ads and pages related to the content of your messages.

2. Hard-copy storage

If you want to store hard (paper) copies, you can simply file sermons and illustrations according to the dates you preached them.

- One easy way to store hard copies of sermons is to print them on half sheets of paper. These easily tuck into your Bible while you're preaching. When you're finished, store each sermon in a 6x9 envelope. Attach your outline and any note-taking sheet you provided for your congregation to the outside of the envelope. At the top right-hand corner, write the date and where you preached the sermon. You might also want to enclose a bulletin from the service, as well as a few notes that can serve as an evaluation if you use the message again.
- Another way to store hard copies is to keep them in three-ring binders. Create a binder for each year, and use tabs for months of sermons and illustrations.

Of course, if you file hard copies by date, you need a way to find sermons based on specific Bible passages or themes. The simplest method is to create a list of all your sermons. Place three columns at the top of a page for the date, Scripture passage, and sermon title or subject. (See the "Sermons Preached" form on page 50.) Each week, simply fill in the information for quick future reference.

No matter how you file hard copies, be sure to protect them from accidental damage. With any manual system, the best approach is to invest in a fire-proof filing cabinet or safe.

3. Hybrid—electronic and hard-copy storage

If you don't have any filing or storage system in place for your sermons, combining both hard copies and electronic copies might be the ultimate way to organize your materials.

- Organize your sermons and illustrations on your computer using two primary folders ("sermons" and "illustrations") and multiple subfolders for dates, Scripture passages, and topics as described above.
- Place hard copies in notebooks, and create the list with date, Scripture passage, and sermon title or subject.

Now you're able to search electronically or browse manually. In addition, with the hard copies in a notebook that represents a whole year of sermons, you can look back to see what books of the Bible you've preached on or what themes you've covered during a particular year.

Sermons Preached

Date	Scripture Passage	Title/Subject

12 Tips on Gestures and Body Language

Experts say that using gestures and body language accounts for more communication than the words you use. If you stand slack, unmoving, and unfeeling before your congregation, you probably won't command much attention. But a few powerful gestures can give passion and immediacy to your message.

How do you develop good gestures and body language? Consider the following ideas.

1. Study the gesturing and body language of good speakers

When you hear another pastor deliver an effective and compelling message, study the speaker's actions. Analyze how effective gestures enhance the message. You can also study poor speakers and note how their body language or lack of gestures detract from the message. You can also purchase videotapes or DVDs of preachers you admire. Study how these pastors use their faces and bodies as they preach.

2. Study yourself on video

Perhaps a speech or preaching professor evaluated your preaching in college or seminary. But you can take it a step further. Have your sound/video technician video your sermon, and then sit in your auditorium and watch yourself on video. Observe how you look to your congregation. How do you compare with other pastors who preach well?

If you can afford it, hire a professional speaking trainer to watch the videos and analyze your style and delivery. A trainer can help you use your own natural style and mannerisms to improve your sermons.

3. Recruit a critique group

Assemble a group of people that can give a viewers' response to your message. Give them a checklist to help them zero in on all aspects of your message, or provide a comment form to focus on what they need to tell you.

4. Practice in the mirror

A variation on this old technique includes saying different prepared lines with different gestures. Determine which delivery is most effective. Practicing in the mirror enables you to try different ways of striking a point to "make it stick." As you hone your message, you might discover certain lines or words that work best with specific gestures.

5. Join a speech-giving group

Join your local ministerial organization or a group like Toastmasters to get feedback on gestures and body language. Toastmasters enables members to give speeches nearly every meeting. Trained evaluators will analyze your speeches in a number of areas, including body language and gestures.

Keep in mind that Toastmasters is a secular group. You can speak on any subject, but a steady diet of warmed-over sermons could irritate other group members. Take the opportunity to develop a variety of messages that you can use in many contexts, such as senior adult groups, men's groups, women's groups, and others.

6. Match your gestures to your setting

In smaller venues—such as a classroom or chapel—be careful not to use broad gestures. In a small room, you can easily look like a lunatic if you shout and overdramatize. However, in larger spaces and with more people, wider gestures are necessary. Get your hands all the way out there when you use a sweeping gesture. Practice using your fingers to make points as you fully extend your arms.

7. Study and use drama in your body language

Add some drama as you speak. Stomp, sashay, swivel, and kick when appropriate. Act out what you're talking about, and your listeners will not only be informed but glued to every word.

8. Coordinate gestures with your voice

Your lips, tongue, throat, and larynx (voice box) are amazing tools of communication. You can shout, whisper, wheedle, threaten, or create any number of other sounds to captivate your listeners. Work at varying your speech. Refuse to use a monotone, droning on like an airplane engine. Instead, use varied ranges in volume to whisper, to be conversational, and to yell when appropriate. And don't forget the power of a pause. When you suddenly stop, eye your congregation, and wait for just a beat or two, they'll be wondering what will happen next.

9. When necessary, use noise

You don't want to pound the pulpit, but sometimes a good whack will wake up the slumbering masses. Even if your congregation is doing its best to pay attention, sometimes a crisp hand clap or a quick slap on a Bible can quickly and effectively communicate, "*This* point's *really* important! Make sure you *hear* it!"

10. Move it!

Don't confine yourself to the pulpit or even the platform or stage. Step out to the side of the podium. Move around. As you work from point to point, take a few paces to the left or right. Stepping down to the floor level where your congregation is sitting is an effective way to communicate a serious or intimate point. Your congregation will sense a greater vulnerability and closeness to you when there's nothing between you and them.

11. Make eye contact

As you speak, move from face to face in an intimate dance of mental touch-and-go. Don't look far off into the distance or over people's heads—you'll unintentionally look arrogant or pompous. Don't look down at people's feet—you'll appear to be hiding something. Instead, in a small congregation, meet the eyes of each person in the room at least once. In a larger venue, make contact with sections of the audience, and always look directly at someone as you make those connections. This communicates that you're sincere and that you genuinely care about the people in your church.

12. Put it all together

A solid sermon has everything—gestures, body language, facial expressions, eye contact, and so on. A balanced mix of all these techniques, not emphasizing just one or two, will make you a better preacher. Everything must work together, and it all should appear natural. That's where practice helps. Take every opportunity to speak as a chance to improve your delivery, and you'll become a more effective and compelling preacher.

46 Creative Sermon-Preparation Techniques

If you think of preaching as an art and sermon preparation as an artistic endeavor, you will be able to battle some of the "preacher's perils" (lack of creativity, lack of ideas, panic). The following, practical artistic tips can help boost your creativity in sermon preparation.

Prepare the Canvas

Artists need a clean and balanced surface for creating their art. Your canvas is your own personal life. So start the art of sermon preparation by preparing yourself.

1. Examine your own spiritual heart

First and foremost, are you maintaining your personal walk with the Lord? Are you being sensitive to the leading of the Holy Spirit? Is there anything God wants to teach *you* through your sermons? Is there sin in your life you haven't dealt with or attitudes that are interfering with your spiritual health? Address any issues as you identify them.

2. Develop a wellness team

Include your doctor, a trusted counselor or accountability partner, a friend, and a fitness trainer. Be sure you see these people on a regular basis.

3. Drink plenty of water

Good hydration increases your focus and concentration. Make sure to have plenty of water handy on the days you prepare your sermons.

4. Drive to the country

Breathe some unpolluted air on a regular basis. Taking a drive out into the countryside will help clear your lungs *and* your head.

5. Exercise

Get the blood pumping to your brain *before* you start preparing your sermons. Go for a brisk walk or bike ride an hour before you sit down to prepare.

6. Eat well

Consume energy-giving foods, including vegetables and fresh fruits, the day before you prepare your sermons.

7. Deal with conflict

Unresolved conflict distracts you from sermon preparation, both mentally and spiritually. Deal with it beforehand.

8. Get out

Give yourself permission to go out with friends. See a movie. Play a round of golf. Get out and have a life.

9. Have a family night once a week

Keeping your family life in balance will balance you as a preacher.

CROSS REFERENCE: Also see Section 5: Recharging Your Personal and Family Life, starting on page 104.

10. Take off at least one day per week

Tell a good friend how you spend your days off each week to ensure that you're not "just doing a few things around the office."

Gain Focus

Focus is important to good art and good sermon preparation. These techniques will help you discover the big ah-ha in any passage of Scripture.

11. Look for repeated words or concepts

The repetition in the passage you're preaching from often contains the meat of the passage. Be sure to serve it to your congregation.

12. Find emphatic words in the original language

Especially in New Testament Greek, the emphatic words often contain the author's big ah-ha, and you can't go wrong with that. If you're not trained in Greek, hunt down a used copy of *The Discovery Bible* by Gary Hill and Gleason Archer (Moody Press, 1987). The author uses a creative coding system to highlight the Greek emphasis in every passage in the New Testament.

13. Find the central promise or command

These are often terrific themes on which to build your sermon. If God was willing to draw a line in the sand with a promise or command, you can feel secure doing the same.

14. Find a connection to a current event

Tying your passage to today's news is a powerful way to preach! However, be sure that God—not the media or your opinions about it—has the last word on these events.

15. Find a tie to Christ's life and work

When putting together your message, be sure to ask yourself, "Did Jesus ever say this, do this, talk about this, or fulfill this?" If Jesus did it, it's probably OK for you to do it, too.

16. Look for a life question the passage answers

If you look hard enough, every verse in Scripture can relate to some aspect of today's life.

17. Look for an attribute of God

Ask yourself, and your congregation, "What does this passage say about God's character?"

18. Ask the Holy Spirit to guide you

What does the Spirit want to say to your congregation through you and through the passage? Never underestimate the Spirit's ability to guide you and your congregation "into all truth" (John 16:13).

Find Inspiration

Artists find inspiration in the world around them. Similarly, you need constant inspiration to fuel the preparation of sermons. Consider the following ideas to find new inspiration for your sermons.

19. Watch a movie

CROSS REFERENCE: Also see "10 Ready-to-Use Movie Illustrations," Section 1, page 23.

Look for spiritual themes in movies. While they often portray unbiblical values, films also illustrate many attitudes and issues people face today. These can serve as good illustrations or present relevant topics to preach on in the future.

20. Listen to other preachers

You can listen to sermons online at www.oneplace.com. Notice how the best preachers set up their sermons and how they move from point to point. Listen to how they illustrate points and how they apply Scripture to contemporary life.

21. Read, read, read

Reading ensures a continual infusion of thoughts and inspiration. If you don't have time to read, check out www.christianbooksummaries.com for free condensations of many Christian books.

22. Practice diversion

Do something unrelated to sermon preparation. New experiences can bring new inspiration. You might try gardening, cooking, quilting, flower arranging, woodworking, pottery, fishing, or hunting. You may very well find spiritual principles illustrated in places you weren't even looking.

23. A change of scenery

Go to a park, to the library, or just another room in the church building. Invest in a notebook computer—the portability allows you to prepare sermons anywhere in the world.

24. Engage in conversation

Talking and articulating your thoughts to others can inspire your whole thinking process. Try getting together with other pastors to talk about what they're preaching on this week.

25. Read the Bible devotionally

Let God's Word inspire you before it's time to write a sermon. Think of reading the Bible as filling a well in your soul that you'll be able to draw from when it's time to prepare your sermons.

26. Get outside your own tradition

Great inspiration awaits in the themes, history, and culture of other church traditions or denominations. Other traditions can bring new life to your messages and ministry. Each year, choose two other church traditions to learn about. Almost all denominations have Web sites with articles and links that present their culture and faith.

27. Live a full life

Don't be a recluse. Participate in family and community activities. Get a hobby. Go out with some friends. Living a full life adds texture and dimension to your preparation. Use your experiences in these areas of your life as illustrations in your sermons.

CROSS REFERENCE:

Also see "2 Self-Directed Retreats," Section 5, page 112.

28. Take a spiritual retreat

Take a personal retreat at a retreat center or even at a monastery. Require yourself, your staff, and key lay leaders to take a personal retreat each quarter.

Awaken Your Senses

Artists realize that a connection exists between the senses and the brain. Learning to awaken your senses helps you stay fresh and energetic in your sermon-preparation time. The following fun activities can help your sermon preparation become more sense-oriented.

29. Invest in a couple pieces of good art

Give yourself something beautiful to look at when you look up from the computer screen in your study. Take down those stuffy college degrees and ordination certificates, and hang artwork with either vivid colors or significant metaphorical meaning.

30. Play music

The right kind of music can awaken your senses and sustain your joy in sermon preparation. Pop a CD into your computer or CD player and fill your office with sound. Pick something like jazz that's lively and complex, or listen to a nature CD to center your senses in God's creation.

31. Smell something pleasant

Smells affect mood and concentration. Citrus and floral scents are most stimulating, herbal scents are relaxing, while heavy food smells make you sleepy. Cut up a lemon or an orange and place the slices in a bowl on your desk. The light citrus smell will fill the room and tell your brain, "It's time to work."

32. Get your hands on it

Touching things can stimulate your awareness of the three-dimensional world that God has made, as well as help you add a sense of earthiness to your sermons. Keep some "natural" items nearby that you can easily pick up and touch. Hold a polished stone, a pine cone, a real sponge, or a seashell. As you touch the world God created, you'll feel more in tune as you prepare to preach.

Sketch Your Sermon

A good painting begins with a good sketch. And good sermons begin with great outlines. The following ways can help you get past the blank page and jump-start your sermon outlining.

33. Create a mind map

On a blank sheet of paper or a large flip chart, write the big ah-ha of your sermon in the center. Then draw lines radiating out from the main idea each connecting to a supporting thought. Combing outlining with drawing enhances your brain's ability to create new ideas and see connections. You can even purchase software to mind-map on your computer. Check out www.mind-map.com for more information.

34. Develop a color-code system

Color-code your outline using highlighters. Select a color for each kind of element in your sermon. For example, shade doctrinal points yellow, application points blue, exegetical points orange, and illustration points green. This helps you to visualize your sermon and make sure it's balanced.

35. Visualize the color of your sermon

Take color-coding one step further by visualizing a color that captures the mood of the Bible passage or your sermon topic. Focusing on color rather than words triggers fresh creativity in the brain. For example, if you're preaching on heaven, visualize bright white or deep jewel colors. Seeing the colors of a topic helps you choose appropriate words and establishes highly creative thought patterns. If you're a visual learner, this is an especially effective technique.

36. Start at the end

Instead of starting at the beginning in your outline, start with the conclusion and work backward. Ask yourself, "Where do I want to lead my congregation in this sermon?" Then ask yourself, "OK, how do I get them there?"

37. Write your sermon in one paragraph

Instead of trying to outline your entire sermon first, capture your sermon in one paragraph. It's much easier to flesh out a summary than to create something out of nothing.

38. Find the "to know" and the "to do"

If you're struggling to put together an outline of your sermon, create two columns on a piece of paper. Label one "To Know" and the other "To Do." In the "To Know" column write down everything that the passage tells us we need to know. What are the facts? In the "To Do" column write down all imperatives. What are we being told to do? A great sermon includes some from each column.

39. Connect the dots

Write down three to five points relating to the overall theme of your sermon with a line space between each point. In the space under each point, write a transition sentence that will lead to the following point. Connecting the thoughts adds clarity and flow to your sermon, so create it right up front.

40. Play Trinity baseball

On a piece of newsprint, draw a baseball diamond with four squares, one each on first, second, and third bases, and at home plate. Now ask yourself, "What does this Bible passage teach about God the Father?" Write that at first base. "What does it teach about God the Son?" Write that at second base. "What does it say about the Holy Spirit?" Write that at third base. Then ask, "How does this passage encourage fellowship with the Triune God?" Write that at home plate. You've just created the outline for a grand slam sermon.

Autograph Your Work

Artists autograph their works in different ways. Some simply sign their work, but others use a unique brush stroke or technique in their creations. Preaching is truth mediated through personality. So as a way of autographing your work, use the following ways to let your personality show in your sermons.

41. Reflect your dominant gifts

Preach from your spiritual gifting. If your spiritual gifts are encouragement and mercy, be sure to preach from that spiritual voice. Include words and thoughts that reflect your gifts. This doesn't mean that you'll only preach on themes related to encouragement and mercy. Instead, keep in mind that your gifts are your core, your vantage point, and most likely the source of your most powerful preaching.

42. Use a key word or phrase regularly

Find a simple phrase (or a collection of phrases) that identifies you and your sermons. You could begin each sermon by praying, "Lord, speak to us—your servants are listening." Or always bridge to the application of your sermons by saying, "So, how then shall we live?" Or conclude every sermon by saying, "The Word of God for the people of God." However God has stamped *you*—that's how you can stamp your preaching of his Word.

43. Preach personal sermons

Preach an annual "State of the Church" sermon. Or on the last Sunday of each year, deliver a sermon on "What I've Learned This Year." On the first Sunday of January, preach a sermon on "What I Envision for Our Church This Year." Or share your personal story of what God has done in your life on or near your birthday each year. Or preach a sermon called "Mistakes I've Made"—share practical lessons you've learned concerning life and faith through failure. Your transparency will speak more to your congregation than your theology (although you'll want to keep that straight, too).

44. Employ a preaching theme

Develop an overarching theme that flavors all your sermons. This could be a doctrinal theme or a practical theme. What is the ultimate goal of all your preaching? Make sure your sermons reflect that goal.

RECOMMENDED RESOURCE:

Looking for that "one thing" in your preaching? Find it in *The 1 Thing: What Everyone Craves—That Your Church Can Deliver,* by Thom and Joani Schultz (Group).

45. Establish a unique spirituality of sermon preparation

Find a few disciplines that you always practice before and after preparing sermons. Sit in silence for a few minutes before and after you prepare to hear God's voice. Or read portions of Psalm 119 aloud to remind yourself of the value of God's Word. Perhaps you'll always fast the day before you prepare your sermon to increase your appetite for God's Word. Or sing a few songs of praise and worship to tune your heart to God's heart. These disciplines will mark your sermon preparation with your unique spirituality.

46. Be yourself

God made you, and you delight him. While preaching, don't bury your personality or perspectives behind a mask. As you prepare your sermons, strive toward authenticity. It will show when you preach.

Section 3:
Revitalizing Your Church's Worship

Your sermon is set to go, but if you're a typical pastor, you also have to concern yourself with the rest of the worship service. How do you teach new worship songs? How do you infuse freshness into your church's prayer life? What can you do with a tired worship space when you have no budget for redecorating?

This section answers these questions and more with dozens of ideas that will help you deepen and strengthen your congregation's times of worship.

Section 3: Table of Contents

21 Creative Ways to Get Others Involved in Worship

Attending a worship service isn't meant to be like a trip to the theater, with audience members passively watching the "show" going on upfront. Worshippers are participants. And not just adults. People of all ages should be actively involved in the experience of worshipping God together. The following ideas offer unique experiential ways you can help all ages of your church family get actively involved in worship.

1. From the mouths of babes

Let the youngest members of your church family set an example of worship and praise! Ask the preschool Sunday school teachers to interview a few children in their classrooms by asking them questions about God, such as "What's something really great about God?" "What is God like?" or "Why do you love God?" Videotape the children's answers. Start your service by reading Matthew 18:1-5, and say: **As we begin our worship today, let's take a moment to listen to the praises of some of the children in our church family.** Show the video, and then continue with your worship service.

2. A monument of thankfulness

Replace some singing time in your worship service with a unique hands-on activity or praise. Set buckets filled with small stones at the entrance of your sanctuary and have ushers tell worshippers to take a stone as they enter the worship area. You can purchase stones like these at home-improvement stores or gardening nurseries. Set one or two permanent markers on the floor beneath each row or pew.

At some point during the worship service, ask participants to reflect on something God has done for them recently that they're thankful for. Invite them to use a marker to write a word or phrase on their stones representing what they're thankful for. Then ask worshippers to tell one other person what they wrote on their rocks and to explain what they're thankful for.

Say: **Many times in the Old Testament, God's people built an altar of stones to commemorate something God had done for them. We have much to be thankful for—let's create a visual symbol representing the many things God has done for us!** Invite worshippers to come to the front and place their stones in a pile to represent an altar. When all the stones have been piled up, lead the congregation in a prayer of gratitude.

3. God-focused graffiti

Hang up several large newsprint banners around the worship area and place markers on the floor in front of each one. At the start of the worship service, point out the banners and explain that while your congregation spends time worshipping God in song, they can go to one of the banners and write or draw prayers and praises to God. Keep the "graffiti walls" and markers out for several weeks so that participants can continue to add prayers and images of praise and worship.

4. Sermons in action

Help your church family develop a life-application mind-set by including a three-minute segment in each worship service when members share how they applied the previous week's sermon to their lives. Ask for volunteers a week in advance so that those sharing will remember to intentionally apply a principle from the sermon to their lives and prepare and practice telling a short summary of how applying God's Word to their lives made a difference in their week.

5. Get 'em gabbing

People love to talk! Capitalize on this innate desire to communicate by including small-group interaction in your worship services. Simply have worshippers form spontaneous small groups with three to five others sitting nearby. You could ask those in the groups to each share a prayer request and then pray silently for each other. Another idea would be to invite participants to discuss an open-ended question at the start of your sermon, such as "What do you think is the biggest problem in society?" or "What are some of the common opinions about Jesus in the world today?"

6. Teens can teach, too

Recruit interested teenagers to prepare and lead a children's sermon during a worship service. Give them a theme (one that ties in with your sermon) and a few ideas for how to make a children's sermon fun, such as including an object lesson, giving kids treats or stickers, using drama or puppets, and having kids do an active experience.

7. Underground prayer

Enlist a team of volunteers to participate in an underground prayer team—truly underground. Two to five members of the prayer team meet in the church basement (or somewhere else behind the scenes, if your church doesn't have a basement) during each worship service and spend the entire time praying for the service. Have them ask God to work through the musicians and worship leaders, to speak through the preacher's sermon, and to work in the lives of visitors who are hearing about God for the first time. Underground prayer-team members should rotate this responsibility so they can also participate in worship services.

8. Listen to your visitors

Make sure that those who come to visit your church not only receive prayer and hear God's Word, but also have the opportunity to let you know what they thought of your worship service. Incorporate their feedback into your future services where it's appropriate to do so. (See the "Visitor Comment and Response" sheet on page 67.)

9. "Yes, Jesus Loves Me"

Select a children's worship song (such as "Jesus Loves Me," "I've Got the Joy," or "This Little Light of Mine"), and make it part of your worship service. Invite a children's Sunday school class to lead the congregation in singing and celebrating Jesus' love. The children will be excited to hear one of their favorite songs being sung by the "big people," and adults will benefit from this easy reminder of childlike praise.

10. Poetry as prayer

Invite creative teenagers or college students to write poems of worship. The students can read poems between worship songs, or you can print their poetry in the bulletin for church members to read silently during a meditative time of the service.

11. Steps-of-faith aisle runner

Ask teenagers or upper-elementary-aged kids to create a cloth or paper aisle runner. Invite them to draw images that represent steps of faith. During a worship service, the students can unroll the aisle runner at the end of the sermon so that it covers the central aisle in the sanctuary. Ask congregation members to exit the service by walking on the steps-of-faith aisle runner. Challenge them to quietly look at the images on the aisle runner and pray about the steps of faith they plan to take during the coming week.

Visitor Comment and Response

Your first impressions   ___ Positive   ___ Negative

Your feelings during worship   ___ Comfortable   ___ Uncomfortable

Greeted warmly?   ___ Yes   ___ No

Were you drawn to worship?   ___ Yes   ___ No

Would you return?   ___ Yes   ___ No

Did you enjoy the music?   ___ Yes   ___ No

Was the sermon helpful?   ___ Yes   ___ No

Did you feel supported by prayer?   ___ Yes   ___ No

The style of worship   ___ Comfortable   ___ Uncomfortable

Your religious background: _____

How did you hear about our church?_____

Would you like to participate in a small group? ____ Yes ____ No

Would you like to be contacted by the pastor? ____ Yes ____ No

Comments:_____

_____

_____

_____

Name (optional): _____

12. Accounts of God's faithfulness

Those in your congregation who've lived a long life are a treasure—and their many experiences of God's faithfulness through the years can be inspiring to all ages of Christians! Recruit a senior adult to share a three- to five-minute story from his or her life during a Sunday morning service, focusing on a specific time when that person experienced God's faithfulness.

13. Church family mosaic

Before a worship service, place a triangle of felt fabric (about six inches in length), a black fabric marker, and a bottle of fabric glue underneath each pew or row. Include several different colors of felt. Then during the service, replace the time of greeting with a time focused on helping the church family connect in fellowship. Tell the congregation they've got three minutes to gather with everyone sitting in their row. (If there aren't others sitting near them, ask them to join another group.) Worshippers should share their names, ages, and interests with others in their group, and everyone should make an effort to memorize what they've learned about each other.

Then have worshippers look under their pew or row for their cloth triangle and marker. Instruct them to work together to write the first name of each person in their group on the piece of felt. Finally, invite a person from each group to affix the felt triangles to a blank cloth banner using fabric glue. The resulting mosaics will each be unique! Later, hang the banners around the sanctuary to represent the beauty and diversity of your church family.

14. "Ministry moment"

Each week, include a "Ministry moment" to focus on a local ministry involving one or more members from your congregation. These could be ministries within the church (children's Sunday school teachers, youth ministry, counseling ministry, the food pantry, the church library) or ministries outside of the church (a local crisis pregnancy center, a soup kitchen, literacy volunteers). Someone who participates in the ministry can briefly tell the congregation some basics and also share one exciting way that God is at work.

15. Make church "cool"

Recruit interested teenagers and college-aged students to form a "media relevancy" team. Give them the job of helping you make church "cool." Regularly provide the team with a list of upcoming sermon topics and Scripture passages, and invite them to give you ideas for movie clips and popular songs that you can use to provoke discussion or illustrate a sermon point. Be sure to actually use some of their ideas!

CROSS REFERENCE:
Also see "10 Ready-to-Use Movie Illustrations," Section 1, page 23.

16. Young readers of the Word

Ask Sunday school teachers to help you identify children who are good readers, and then contact their parents to see if those kids would like to read Scripture during a worship service. Assign children short and simple passages and request that parents practice with the children throughout the week. Then give them a microphone and let them share God's truth with the congregation.

17. Incorporate responsive readings

Creating a responsive reading is as simple as compiling meaningful Scripture passages that all relate to a central theme. Assign various groups—men, women, teenagers, parents, grandparents, left of the center aisle, right of the center aisle—to read different parts. The congregation reads it aloud as if they're reading a script. This will keep worshippers on their toes as they figure out when it's their turn to read.

18. More than just a craft

Every so often, ask children's Sunday school teachers to give you drawings that children have made during craft time. Select a drawing that will photocopy well, and then ask the child's (and parents') permission to use it as the cover of a worship bulletin. During the service, thank the child for worshipping God through art and for allowing you to use the drawing to help adults in the church praise God.

19. New flowers for new babies

Celebrate the arrival of new babies in your church family by placing a rose in a vase at the front of the church following the baby's birth. While a newborn's mother probably won't be at the service, if the father is present, invite him to come to the front and receive the rose as the congregation celebrates the good news with applause. Be sure to take a moment to lead the congregation in prayer for the family.

20. Prayer-and-praise board

Set up a dry-erase board (with dry-erase markers and an eraser) in the back of your worship area with the words "Prayers and Praises" at the top. Invite worshippers to visit the dry-erase board before or after worship services, where they can list nonconfidential requests for others to pray for. Whenever a prayer is answered, worshippers can erase the request and replace it with a praise—a short description of how God worked in the situation. Regularly reinforce the idea that sharing your prayers and praises is an important aspect of worshipping together.

21. Scripture meditation

Practice Scripture meditation as a congregation by selecting a short Bible verse and printing it in the bulletin. During your worship service, lead the congregation in reading the verse in unison several times. Then ask worshippers to take two or three minutes to quietly reflect and pray about the meaning of the verse in their lives.

9 Ideas for Informal Worship

As you lead your congregation, remember that worship shouldn't be reduced to what happens during a Sunday morning service. Worship is a lifestyle that affects everything you do! By adding informal worship gatherings with different-sized groups, you can begin to bring worship out of its "church building" box. Some of the following suggestions work with any size group, while others work with 10 or fewer people.

1. At the water

(Any size) Gather at a local river, lake, pond, stream, or ocean shore. Read a passage about water, such as an Old Testament story (creation, "well-courtship" narratives such as Jacob's, the parting of the sea, water coming from the rock), or a narrative from Jesus' life (baptism, calming the sea, the woman at the well). Select related music, and worship together. In addition, an outdoor baptism in a real body of water is always a moving event.

2. In the park

(Any size) Rather than meeting inside during the summer, gather at a local park. Bring along a few chairs for older folks to sit on; others can sit on blankets or mats on the grass. Choose music everyone knows, so you don't have to worry about printed material. Focus on the glory of creation and the Creator's imagination.

3. Along a street

(Any size) Meeting on the side of a street is a very public event, but it can also draw people into your church. Check with your local community government about regulations so that people aren't illegally crowding the sidewalks. As an alternative, you could meet on a church member's front yard in a moderately busy neighborhood. Plan the service with multiple "entry points" (a lot of singing, activities for worshippers, short meditations rather than a long sermon) so it's accessible to people who stop while they're walking by. Finish off your time with refreshments.

4. In a parking lot

(Any size) Check with the parking-lot owner for permission to meet. Spend time praying for the surrounding businesses and housing developments. Pray for safety for the people driving, for ethical business in the surrounding shops. Read the Creation narrative, a praise psalm, or a lament together. Sing a song like "For the Beauty of the Earth" or "Let All Things Now Living" in response to your surroundings.

5. At a field

(Any size) Get permission from a farmer to gather next to a field. Perhaps the farmer could talk about the crop being raised. Sing a song of thanksgiving to God for the food he provides. If it's OK with the owner, encourage people to walk through the field and pray silently.

6. In a restaurant

(Medium-to-small group) Meet together for a meal. Take time to eat and visit with one another. Pray or sing before each course. Focus upon God's gift of food. For an excellent introduction to a theology of food, browse through *Food for Life: The Spirituality and Ethics of Eating,* by L. Shannon Jung (Fortress Press, 2004).

7. Communion with friends

(Medium-to-small group) Make a whole meal of communion. Fill up your dining room table with people, and bring out the bread and wine or grape juice as the first course. Read the Last Supper narrative together (Luke 22:7-38). Encourage people to take large pieces of bread and put butter or olive oil on them. Give each person a whole glass of juice or wine. Really *commune* together!

8. With crafts

(Any size) Some people like to keep their hands moving all the time. Put together a special worship service where crafts and handiwork are welcome. People can sit, listen, sing, and crochet or whittle while they worship.

9. Under the stars

(Any size) Gather at night in a place dark enough to see the stars and planets. Encourage worshippers to bring blankets and lie on their backs to see the stars. Sing a song of praise. Sense the smallness of yourselves and the largeness of God—yet remind people that God knows each of his children intimately.

8 Ways to Revitalize Your Worship Space

An adage in the theater world says, "Cheap, fast, good—choose two." That's applicable to many things. So as you try each of the following suggestions for breathing new life into a tired worship space, decide if you need it to be inexpensive, quick, or great—and then "choose two."

1. Bring the outside in

Why use artificial flowers with so much natural beauty around? Ask an individual or a group of people to create beautiful displays of sticks, leaves, plants, vegetables and fruits, shells, stones, and other natural materials to decorate your worship space. If it fits with the theme of your service, recruit some volunteers to hand out similar God-created pieces for the congregation to hold during the service.

2. Ask an expert

Perhaps someone in your congregation has a knack for arranging things—chairs, decorations, artwork. Ask this individual to assist in redesigning the elements already present in your worship space. Set a small budget, allow the interior designer to make a plan (you don't want three of your four walls painted in primary colors), and set to work. Maybe you can't afford new carpet, but with some repainted walls and rearranged furniture, maybe the carpet won't stick out so much.

3. Use local artists

Give several artists a theme and see what they come up with. They could each create a piece of art representing a specific Scripture passage, a story of faith, an aspect of Christian faith, or an event in church history. Imagine the artistic interpretations of spiritual growth, salvation, the coming of the Holy Spirit, or the body of Christ. Or ask a group of artists to work collaboratively to create a grouping of related but diverse pieces. For example, each artist could create a character from the manger scene for Christmas. Of course, provide some size guidelines—you don't want to end up with a life-sized baby Jesus and a 12-inch Mary. Or artists could depict different portions of Bible stories for use as illustrations during a sermon.

4. Create banners

Banners can be expensive, but they don't have to be. Rather than ordering banners from a church catalog, simply ask around for artists and people who can sew, and let them express the character of your congregation. Because banners might be displayed for a while, don't select colors and designs that will look dated in a few years. Consider modeling some banners after traditional stained glass—let them tell God's story in color and form!

5. Rearrange the seats

Does the arrangement of the chairs or pews support or contradict your church's message and mission? Is "community" a buzzword at your church? Then examine whether the chair configuration really communicates "community focused" or if it says "pastor focused" instead. If possible, move the seating so that people can see one another without twisting their necks all the way around.

6. Play a game

If everyone sits in the same place week after week, play "Apple Cart Upset"! Get everyone to stand up and move to a new seat— perhaps with the rule that people sit by someone they don't know. You'll revitalize your worship space just by reconfiguring the people! And some might get the idea and do this on their own *every* week.

7. Try background music

No, not sleep-inducing elevator tunes. Instead, break up the routine by having music come from the back of the worship space rather than being the focal point in the front. You might need to adjust the type of music you use, instruments, and vocalists, but it might change your congregation's focus, too.

8. Put on a fancy feast

For a communion service, ask an artistic person to decorate the communion table with beautiful items—silver candleholders and a white tablecloth, ethnic cloths and baskets full of bread, or all different shapes and sizes of pottery goblets. Communion is a celebration, so let the table *look* like you're celebrating! The table can look different each time you celebrate communion—one time traditionally elegant, another time celebrating the ethnic culture of your community or congregation.

10 Ideas for Using Other Elements in Worship

If someone asked you to describe your church's worship time, would the word "creative" be part of your answer? It's easy to fall into a rut with worship. But the problem with a rut is that when you go over and over the same path, the rut just gets deeper. Use the following ideas to infuse some freshness into your worship times—simply by introducing some unexpected items and situations into your services.

1. Two plants

The first kind of plant is a real plant. Living plants bring God's creation into your worship space. Your congregation will be able to see the plant's growth from week to week. Ask someone with a green thumb to take care of the plant during the week, especially if your worship space has limited sunshine. Use the plant as an opportunity to talk about growth in Christ.

The second plant is a "plant"—someone placed in your congregation to add an element of surprise during the worship service. The "plant" might ask a question during your sermon or respond to a prayer in a physical way.

2. Flags

Although many churches have flags at the front of their worship space, you can use these elements beyond having someone dust them weekly and clean them every few years. Use a variety of international flags to celebrate Pentecost. Invite people to enter the worship area in procession, waving the flags, and shouting praises to God in diverse languages. Or display a different international flag each week, and provide information so worshippers can pray for that country and/or for missionaries located there.

3. Children

Children can add much more to worship than singing a cute song. Ask children to read the Scripture. Better, ask them to act out the story. For example, in the story of the dry bones in Ezekiel 37:1-14, some children can portray the bones by lying still on the stage. Others can be the noise and the breath moving among the bones as they wave ribbons and streamers behind them. Finally, the bones can slowly stand up and march together like an army off the stage. Other passages that work well with children include:

- the Creation narrative (Genesis 1:1–2:3)
- the tower of Babel (Genesis 11:1-9)
- the Israelites crossing the sea (selected portions of Exodus 13:17–15:21)
- the river of life (Revelation 22:1-6)

This works best when the children move rather than talk. Invite a creative leader to help determine movements and rehearse with the children.

4. Dancers

In addition to interpretive solo movement, dancers can also act out portions of Scripture. Other ways to incorporate dance include:

- Ask a dancer or group of dancers to "dance in" the Bible, celebrating the gift of God's Word through movement.
- Dance doesn't portray just happy or celebratory moments. For a Good Friday service, a dancer can creatively use movement to drape a black cloth around the cross while "O Sacred Head, Now Wounded" or "What Wondrous Love Is This?" plays as an accompaniment.
- In some African countries, people dance their offerings to the front of the meeting place to celebrate the honor of giving to God.

Some people might be uncomfortable watching dance during worship. Hold a "dance workshop" to help worshippers understand the beauty, praise, and love expressed to God that can come from such movement.

5. Scripture reading

How often is Scripture read during your service? Use the following ways to incorporate more Scripture readings into your worship times.

- At the beginning of your service, ask people to stand for the presentation of the Scripture. Have children, youth, or adults take turns bringing in the Bible and placing it on the pulpit or on a table in front of your worship area. This practice demonstrates the centrality of God's Word in your service.
- Read responsively. This works well for the Psalms and other poetry. Use pew Bibles or project the Scripture reading on a screen so that everyone reads the same translation.

- Encourage people to bring their Bibles to church. Make sure you honor this action by asking worshippers to open their Bibles for Scripture readings and your sermon.
- Use more than one Scripture reading. Select related passages from several portions of Scripture: Old Testament history books, the prophets, the Psalms or other poetry books, the Gospels, and the epistles.

6. Different-colored banners

Banners can serve as a great worship focus in your space. Incorporate different traditional colors that represent the church year into banners. These colors include blue for Advent, gold for Christmas, green for Epiphany, purple for Lent, red for Holy Week, gray or black for Good Friday, white or gold for Easter, red for Pentecost, and green for the season after Pentecost. Check the following Web sites for descriptions of the symbolism of the liturgical colors and how to use them in worship:

- www.cyberfaith.com/liturgical_year.cfm
- www.cresourcei.org/symbols/colorsmeaning.html

7. Diversity

When planning a service, consider how your congregation is represented. For example, if a visitor attends your service and sees people of a single gender or race leading in worship, what does it communicate about the diversity of your congregation? Even if your congregation doesn't have much racial diversity, involve both men and women in your service. (Also see the "Worship Planning Guide" form on page 78.)

8. Scents

Involve the sense of smell in worship. If you're speaking about bread (Jesus as the bread of life, communion, manna in the wilderness), set a bread machine so that bread is baking during your talk. Or if you're talking about spices (the gifts of the wise men, embalming spices), do the old holiday trick of setting up a Crock-Pot with water and spices (cinnamon, cloves, orange peel, cardamom pods, coriander seeds) to add scent to the air.

Worship Planning Guide

Date of service: _____

Opening hymns: _____

Worship & Praise choruses: _____

Closing hymn/chorus: _____

Worship leaders: _____

Other musicians: _____

Special music: _____

Drama: _____

Participants: _____

Sermon title: _____

Scripture passages: _____

Audio-visual and PowerPoint use: _____

A-V Technician: _____

Sound needs: _____

Sound technician: _____

Miscellaneous Information: _____

_____

_____

9. Lighting

Adjust the lighting to match the mood of the service. Dim the lights to emphasize that corporate worship time also involves a personal connection between the worshipper and God. Similarly, turn up the lights to celebrate the community of faith by allowing people to see one another. Use stage-lighting gels over the lights to change the mood in other ways.

10. The Christmas tree

At Christmastime, make decorating the church tree a part of your worship time. Make it a missionary tree by hanging prayer cards or photographs of missionaries, along with small envelopes for worshippers to fill with financial gifts for missionaries. Or create a tree for the homeless by filling the tree with gifts of scarves, mittens, and hats throughout the season. Worshippers can also donate shampoo, toothpaste, and other personal items, placing them under the tree. Just before Christmas, donate the items to a local homeless shelter.

18 Innovative Ways to Introduce New Songs to Your Congregation

Some people love the novelty of learning new songs. Others would prefer to stick to their old favorites. As you raise the idea of learning new worship songs, refer to Scripture passages that mention a "new song" or "new songs" (Psalms 33:3; 40:3; 96:1; 98:1; 144:9; 149:1; Isaiah 42:10; Revelation 5:9; 14:3). Then use the following ideas to make new songs into new favorites.

1. Play it as background music

For a week or two before the congregation learns a song, ask the musician(s) to play the music before, during, or after the service to familiarize people with the melody.

2. Utilize the text

Consider the genre of the song's text. Is it a prayer? a statement of belief? Does it proclaim God's glory? Find a place in your service where the words of the song fit, display the text on a large screen or print it in the bulletin, and direct the congregation to *read* (not sing) the words together as corporate prayer, affirmation, or blessing.

3. Gospel-style "call and response"

Some songs work naturally with this style, especially ones that repeat individual lines of music. Ask a singer to lead the congregation in the following way: The leader will sing a line of music, gesturing to the congregation to repeat the same exact line. If you're up for a bigger challenge, you can sing most any song or hymn in this manner. (Think about the hymn "Holy, Holy, Holy." After a leader sings the first line, "Holy, holy, holy! Lord God Almighty!" the congregation simply echoes it.) For this method to work, you really need a strong vocalist the congregation trusts.

4. Repetition, repetition, repetition

This is not to say that you should sing the song a dozen times in a row! Repeat but with different versions. Ask your praise band or organist to play the song for a prelude. Then, sing the new piece as the second song in your worship time. Later, sing it again—perhaps as a closing, so people can sing it as they exit.

5. Encourage home singing

To learn a new song quickly, urge individual families to sing it as a prayer before a meal. Sing the song once during your worship service, and then provide lyrics (and music, for families who can read it) so that people can practice at home. Sing it at your service the following week. Encourage the congregation whether or not they improve! (Note: Copyright laws might prohibit you from photocopying some music for home use. Check with the copyright holder, or use music in public domain.)

6. Do a "Hymns of the Faith" study

Teach a Sunday school class that focuses on learning or revisiting old hymns. In addition to singing the hymns in class, focus on the theology of the hymns. People who view hymns as old-fashioned or boring will reconnect when they realize the depth of the theology in the hymns.

7. Learn a new song in a different language

Rather than learning a song first in English, learn it in another language first. Ask someone proficient in the language to teach it to the congregation, and sing it for several weeks. Later, add the English translation alongside the first language. Direct the congregation to sing both languages simultaneously, or to alternate between languages.

8. Use movement

For a new song, ask a choreographer to orchestrate a movement for the congregation to participate in. As the congregation learns new words, they will also learn the corresponding movements.

9. Let the younger teach the older

For a simple song, ask some children's classes or a children's choir to learn the song first. Of course, they'll need at least several weeks' advance notice. Then, during a worship service, have the kids sing while the adults listen. Finally, have them sing together.

10. Utilize your local gifts

If you have a composer or songwriter in your congregation, ask that individual to write a song for your congregation for a special occasion or holiday. People love to learn songs created just for them and their situation! Another option is to ask a poet to write a new text to an old hymn tune or other melody.

11. Sing songs in season

Be aware of what season you're experiencing. Spring, summer, fall? Is it Advent, Easter, or Christmas? Select songs that fit with the year! Sing harvest and thanksgiving songs in the autumn, and songs about the resurrection on and after Easter. If you select a new song and explain why and how it fits with the season, people will be more willing to learn it.

12. Be a singing preacher

No matter what talents you have as a singer, people will listen when you break out in song during your sermon. Of course, the new song needs to fit well with your sermon. When people see you bravely trying something new, they'll willingly join in.

13. Choose a theme song

Theme songs can be seasonal, topical, annual, or permanent. Consider the season, topic, or mission of your church, find several appropriate songs, and try them out with your congregation. Aim for a song of medium length—not too long or too short. Also, try to avoid text and music that people will tire of or start to parody.

14. Keep a goal in mind

Learn a new song for a specific event. Does your church gather annually with other congregations for a local holiday service? Are you inviting missionaries to your church? Welcome them with a new song!

15. Informal pre-service singing

If the room where you worship isn't used before your services, hold a 15-minute singing time before the service begins. This shouldn't take the place of part of the service, but it provides an option for those who want to do additional singing. Sing alternate types of music, sing requested songs, spend time learning new songs, and warm up the vocal chords.

16. Teach the new song's history

When was the song written? Who wrote it? Why? What was the spiritual setting for the song? A good resource for learning about hymns and their writers is www.cyberhymnal.org (most hymns listed on this Web site are public domain; if copyrighted, a notice appears at the top of the specific page).

17. Intersperse preaching with singing

Preach a sermon in parts, using the verses of a new song or hymn between the portions of the message. This keeps people listening and provides an interactive way to worship and preach.

18. Interview children about song meanings

To get people thinking about what they're singing about, ask children what a song means. You can video answers and edit to the most entertaining responses. "What does 'Give me oil in my lamp' mean?" "What does the first line of 'Silent Night' tell us?" This works with a new song or an old song!

12 Interactive Prayer Ideas

Has prayer become a worn-out part of your worship services? Use the following ideas to help your church members find new passion and interest in prayer.

1. Church prayer walk

Ask the congregation to form groups of no more than 10 people. Ask them to leave your worship area, walk around the church, stop at various locations in the church building, and pray for that area of ministry. For example, a group outside the youth room should pray for the needs of the students and for their leaders. Do the same for the children's room, the gym, the church offices, and other areas of the building.

2. Figurative praying

Give each person in the congregation a strip of modeling clay as they enter the worship service. During an extended prayer time, ask people to mold their clay into a symbol that represents a prayer need, and then have a time of silent prayer for individuals to pray about their own needs. You can take this a step further by having members of the congregation share with one other person what their clay represents. When both people have shared, they can pray for each other's needs.

3. Prayer Post-it wall

Pass out Post-it notes as people enter the worship service. During a prayer time, have people write prayer requests on their sticky notes. Then, create a prayer wall by having worshippers stick their requests to the wall—either during or immediately following the service. Put your prayer wall in a corner or in a room with enough space for people to sit or kneel in front of the wall to pray about the needs they see.

4. Interactive prayer stations

Create different stations or scenes around the room. At each station, individuals or small groups read instructions to pray about a certain item—either topically or specifically. For example, at one station, set up a garden display that includes different elements of creation (plants, a goldfish pond, a small "sand box"). Those who gather at this station should thank God for his creation and write in the sand what aspect of creation they're most grateful for. Another station might focus on praising God through prayer, where participants can listen to praise music from a CD there. At another station, participants can use markers, crayons, and paints to create a drawing or painting to remind them of the need to pray.

5. Children's prayer service

Once a month or quarter, recruit children to take part in your prayer time. Let them pray aloud. Their prayers can be surprisingly astute and on the mark.

6. Cross service

Ask a woodworker in your church to create a wooden cross to place at the front of your worship area. If the area already has a cross, this idea can use the permanently installed cross. At the beginning of your worship service, have ushers distribute paper and pens to worshippers. At the end of your worship service or following a time of communion, invite people to come to the front to place their needs, burdens, praises, or intercession at the cross. Worshippers can stay and pray at the foot of the cross as long as they'd like, then return to their seats or leave the service when finished. After the service, destroy the papers to maintain the participants' privacy.

7. Prayers-to-heaven campfire

During an evening service, have volunteers build a large campfire in a cleared area of the church parking lot or another safe location on the church's property. At the end of the service, direct worshippers outdoors. Similar to the cross service above, invite people to write prayers on paper and then to put the papers in the campfire, releasing their prayers to God.

8. Neighborhood prayer walks

At the close of a service, distribute maps of the area around the church property. Divide the area into territories and assign a team to each territory. Each team walks together through the streets of their area, praying for the needs of people in the homes and businesses they pass.

9. Pass it on

Give each worshipper a sheet of paper and ask him or her to write down a request that others can pray for today. Then each person passes the paper to the person on his or her right. Pause to give people time to pray. Then, each person passes the prayer request to the next person on his or her right. Keep passing the prayers around until five or six people have prayed for each request.

10. Popcorn prayers

During your worship service prayer time, say a word, describe a situation, or mention a person's name. Worshippers can pop out one-sentence prayers relating to each topic.

11. Directory-based prayer

Pass out copies of the church directory at the beginning of the service and spend time in silent prayer. Each person should spend time praying for a page of church members. You can spend time praying through school directories, neighborhood directories, nursing-home directories, or local business directories.

12. Sit on it!

Before your worship service, write prayer needs on pieces of paper or sticky notes and affix them to the bottom of the chairs or pews. During your prayer time, have people pull the needs from underneath their chairs and pray for them.

10 Benedictions and Other Creative Service Closings

How do you end your worship services? The following ideas offer great closings to encourage your congregation to leave with a clear mind-set about worship—thinking of Christ and giving thanks for God's great gifts.

1. Variations of Amen

Sing one of the traditional "Amen" variations from a hymnal, or sing the gospel song "Amen." Or create a simple leader-congregation response—whenever you say, "Amen," the congregation responds, "So be it!"

2. Scripture benedictions

The New Testament, especially the epistles, contains great benedictions you can memorize and use to bless your congregation. Consider the following passages:

- Romans 16:25-27;
- 1 Corinthians 16:22b-24;
- 2 Corinthians 13:11b, 14;
- Ephesians 3:14-21;
- Ephesians 6:23-24;
- 1 Thessalonians 5:23;
- 2 Thessalonians 3:16;
- Hebrews 13:20-21;
- 2 Peter 3:18;
- Jude 24-25;
- Revelation 22:17, 20-21.

3. Go out with joy

End the service with an upbeat chorus or hymn. Then repeat the song, encouraging people to joyfully exit the worship space as they continue to sing.

4. The open ending

Instead of ending the service, allow time for silent prayer. Encourage people who leave to exit quietly, and for those who wish to visit, to take their conversation outside the worship area.

5. Imperatives

Finish the service with a declaration to your congregation. Some ideas:

- "Go in peace to love and serve the Lord!"
- "You are the light of the world! Let your light shine among all people!"
- "You are a new creation. Live like the new creation that you are."

6. Small-group prayer

Encourage small groups of three or four worshippers to pray together at the end of your service. Remind people to leave quietly when they're finished praying so other groups can remain focused on their prayer times.

7. Small tokens

CROSS REFERENCE: For more take-away ideas, see Section 4: 20 Worship Service Jump-Starts, starting on page 90.

Pass out small objects as a reminder of the service. Ideas include:

- Light bulbs—you are the light of the world! (You can use the small Christmas light bulbs to save money).
- Seeds or bulbs—grow in Christ!
- Pieces of fabric—to remember Christ's humanity through the story of his birth (swaddling clothes) and crucifixion (cloak). Select a different fabric for each story.

8. Repeat the big idea

Make sure that the end of your service corresponds with the primary topic or theme of the service by repeating the significant song, Scripture passage, or application.

9. Personal application and response

Pass out paper. Invite worshippers to respond personally to the service. Some might choose not to write, but instead pray or leave. Others may want to write a prayer or a response to God on the paper. Encourage people to pray and listen for God's guidance. Provide vessels to collect the paper. Others might want to keep or destroy what they've written. Provide all the options you can think of.

10. Outside

Depending upon your location circumstances, you can end the service outside. Together, sing as you leave the service. Then focus on something outside—creation, the community "mission field," saying a public farewell to someone as he or she drives away, or praying for a much-needed new building.

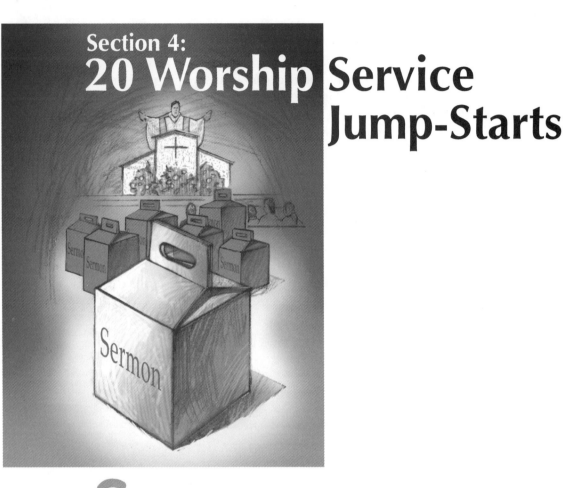

Section 4:
20 Worship Service Jump-Starts

Sometimes you can't get your brain in gear. Yet the weekend is coming and you need to put together a worship service. You can't just tell your congregation how busy you've been, send them home, and urge them to come back next week when you have more time.

Each of the following ideas will help you jump-start your worship planning—even at the last minute. Each idea includes a number of elements, such as a main point for the service and appropriate Scripture and music choices. (Note that the hymns listed here are in public domain. Additional composer/lyric information for contemporary choruses can be found at www.sharesong.org and www.pwarchive.com.)

Use the pieces that fit your church and toss out the rest. But be sure to check out the take-away elements—something to give worshippers to help them recall the service's theme.

Section 4: Table of Contents

4 Services to Spark Fresh Starts

1. A new beginning

Main Point: Renewal and restoration.

Whether it's New Year's Day or the start of just about any season or occasion, you can focus on God's unbelievable offer of renewal and restoration.

Occasions to use: New Year's Eve; New Year's Day; first day of spring; Easter season; first day of summer; back-to-school time

Scripture: "Do not lose heart. Though outwardly we are wasting away, yet inwardly we are being renewed day by day" (2 Corinthians 4:16).

Quote: "To look backward for a while is to refresh the eye, to restore it, and to render it the more fit for its prime function of looking forward."—Margaret Fairless Barber

Hymn: "Another Year Is Dawning"

Contemporary Chorus: "Create in Me a Clean Heart"

Take-away: Magnetic calendars, imprinted with your church logo, will remind worshippers throughout the year of the renewal God offers.

2. Back to school

Main Point: A time of prayer for students and schools.

As you dedicate students to the Lord, keep in mind that students come in all ages—from children facing their first day of kindergarten to a college student facing dorm life to a single adult facing studies after a layoff.

Occasions to use: Late August or early September; after the new year begins

Scripture: "The fear of the Lord is the beginning of wisdom, and knowledge of the Holy One is understanding" (Proverbs 9:10).

Quote: "What we are is God's gift to us. What we become is our gift to God."—Eleanor Powell

Hymn: "Be Thou My Vision"

Contemporary Chorus: "In Your Presence"

Take-away: Give worshippers a #2 pencil as they leave your services as a reminder to pray for children and parents during the school year.

3. Health and fitness

Main Point: Opportunity to conduct a spiritual fitness checkup.
   While our culture often focuses on body image and physical fitness, your service can encourage a spiritual health exam for individuals in your congregation.

Occasions to use: Following Thanksgiving or Christmas (when everyone claims to eat too much); first day of spring; beginning of summer

Scripture: "Those who hope in the Lord will renew their strength. They will soar on wings like eagles; they will run and not grow weary, they will walk and not be faint" (Isaiah 40:31).

Quote: "Family life is full of major and minor crises—the ups and downs of health, success and failure in career, marriage, and divorce—and all kinds of characters. It is tied to places and events and histories. With all of these felt details, life etches itself into memory and personality. It's difficult to imagine anything more nourishing to the soul."—Thomas Moore

Hymn: "Praise Ye the Lord, the Almighty"

Contemporary Chorus: "I'm a Witness"

Take-away: Give out half pints of bottled water as a reminder to stay hydrated while staying physically fit. Remind worshippers that Jesus is the living water that supplies us with what we need to be spiritually fit.

4. Big dreams

Main Point: God's desires for us exceed our wildest dreams.
   Both individually and as a congregation, what are your big dreams? What exciting things does God have in store for you personally? What amazing things will he do with your church?

Occasions to use: New Year's Day; Martin Luther King Jr. Day; annual church business meeting; anytime

Scripture: "Now to him who is able to do immeasurably more than all we ask or imagine, according to his power that is at work within us, to him be glory in the church and in Christ Jesus throughout all generations, for ever and ever! Amen" (Ephesians 3:20-21).

Quote: "Go confidently in the direction of your dreams. Live the life you've imagined."—Henry David Thoreau

Hymn: "Standing on the Promises"

Contemporary Chorus: "Amen" (Bob Fitts)

Take-away: Pass out small containers of confetti, to celebrate big dreams.

5 Ways to Focus on Acts of Service

1. Good neighbors

Main Point: Reach out and invite a neighbor to church.

Remind your congregation of the mission field where we all serve—our neighborhoods.

Occasions to use: Prior to regular and special services during holiday seasons; "Invite-a-Friend Sundays"

Scripture: "No more lies, no more pretense. Tell your neighbor the truth. In Christ's body we're all connected to each other, after all. When you lie to others, you end up lying to yourself" (Ephesians 4:25, *The Message*).

Quote: "It is easier to love humanity as a whole than to love one's neighbor."—Eric Hoffer

Hymn: "Take Time to Be Holy"

Contemporary Chorus: "In Your Presence"

Take-away: Distribute packets of flower seeds that people in your congregation can give to neighbors.

2. Celebrate the harvest

Main Point: Jesus calls us to bring in the harvest of people who don't yet know him.

Harvest time is a great time to be thankful for all that God provides. But Jesus used the image of harvest in another way—to represent unchurched people around us. He sends us out to the fields to "bring them in."

Occasions to use: Any Sunday during autumn/harvest season; missions-emphasis weeks

Scripture: "Open your eyes and look at the fields! They are ripe for harvest" (John 4:35).

Quote: "Give fools their gold, and knaves their power;
Let fortune's bubbles rise and fall;
Who sows a field, or trains a flower,
Or plants a tree, is more than all."—John Greenleaf Whittier

Hymn: "Hark, the Voice of Jesus Calling"

Contemporary Chorus: "We Declare" (Esther B.A. Soon)

Take-away: In the fall, apples are plentiful and inexpensive, and some varieties are available all year. Celebrate the harvest by giving each worshipper an apple at the end of your services. Look for a local orchard to add a unique and local flavor to this giveaway item.

3. Acts of kindness

Main Point: "They will know we are Christians by our love (and our acts of kindness)."

As Christians, the Holy Spirit lives in us and empowers us to do "immeasurably more than all we ask or imagine" (Ephesians 3:20). We should be the leaders in the world when it comes to spreading goodness and kindness.

Occasions to use: Anytime

Scripture: "The fruit of the Spirit is love, joy, peace, patience, kindness, goodness, faithfulness, gentleness and self-control. Against such things there is no law" (Galatians 5:22-23).

Quote: "You cannot do a kindness too soon, for you never know how soon it will be too late."—Ralph Waldo Emerson

Hymn: "Come, Holy Spirit, Heavenly Dove"

Contemporary Chorus: "As for Me and My House"

Take-away: Blue ribbons. You've seen different-colored ribbons tied around old oak trees, magnetic versions on cars to show patriotism, and other colors to represent many different causes. Have ushers distribute lengths of blue ribbon, and encourage worshippers to use them as bookmarks or to tie on their car antennas. Each time they see their ribbons, they should try to think of a simple way to show kindness to another person—even just holding a door for an elderly person or helping a harried mom carry groceries to her car.

4. Serving others

Main Point: God allows us to be his hands and feet and heart to serve and love people around us.

He equips us with spiritual gifts to build up the church and to serve those who don't know him.

Occasions to use: Community service fairs, missions weeks, anytime

Scripture: "Each one should use whatever gift he has received to serve others, faithfully administering God's grace in its various forms" (1 Peter 4:10).

Quote: "Everybody can be great...because anybody can serve." —Martin Luther King Jr.

Hymn: "Our Best"

Contemporary Chorus: "As for Me and My House"

Take-away: Purchase a box of Avery burst labels at an office-supply store. Use an inkjet printer to print a simple message on the labels (most word-processing programs include templates listed by Avery numbers) such as "God's Servant" or "As for Me and My House." Have greeters place a sticker on each person, either when they enter or leave the service.

5. "Least of These" awards

Main Point: Honor the volunteers who carry out the ministries of your church.

Take a cue from an awards show, and celebrate the people in your church who deserve an award more than a Hollywood actor or musician.

Occasions to use: During a weekend when an award show (Emmys, Oscars, Grammys) is telecast; anytime

Scripture: "Serve wholeheartedly, as if you were serving the Lord, not men, because you know that the Lord will reward everyone for whatever good he does" (Ephesians 6:7-8).

Quote: "The greatest reward for doing is the opportunity to do more."—Jonas Salk

Hymn: "Make Me a Blessing"

Contemporary Chorus: "I Have Kept the Faith"

Take-away: Print copies of the "Certificate of Appreciation" found on page 97 (or create your own for a custom and professional look), fill out with volunteers' names and your signature, and distribute to volunteers in your congregation.

Certificate of Appreciation

This award is presented to:

in appreciation of your continued dedication and commitment to serve and minister to others.

Thank You!

Church Name

Date

Pastor

4 Services for Honor and Dedication

1. Honoring children

Main Point: Affirm the children in your church by dedicating them to God and focusing on the importance of their spiritual growth.

Make the commitment that your church will help parents raise healthy and happy children; will cherish the lives of babies; will encourage the success and spiritual formation of every child; and will urge teenagers to pursue their dreams as they discover the excitement and freedom of living in God's will.

Occasions to use: Mother's Day; Father's Day; National Children's Day (the second Sunday in October); child-dedication services; Sunday school promotion week

Scripture: "Don't make your children angry by the way you treat them. Rather, bring them up with the discipline and instruction approved by the Lord" (Ephesians 6:4, *New Living Translation*).

Quote: "Children are the living messages we send to a time we will not see."—John W. Whitehead

Hymn: "Savior, Like a Shepherd Lead Us"

Contemporary Chorus: "Blessed Be Your Name"

Take-away: Give worshippers several pieces of individually wrapped candy. While they're enjoying a sweet snack, ask them to pray for the spiritual growth of the children in your church.

2. Honoring workers

Main Point: Take an opportunity to honor bosses, employees, laborers and other workers.

Use this service to help worshippers focus on the attitude of "working for the Lord."

Occasions to use: Labor Day; "greeting card days" such as National Boss Day or National Secretary's Day

Scripture: "Whatever you do, work at it with all your heart, as working for the Lord, not for men, since you know that you will receive an inheritance from the Lord as a reward. It is the Lord Christ you are serving" (Colossians 3:23-24).

Quote: "Pray as though everything depended on God. Work as though everything depended on you."—Saint Augustine

Hymn: "Not I but Christ"

Contemporary Chorus: "Surrender"

Take-away: Give each worshipper a penny to represent working and earning a living. Whenever they see a penny, they can pray that God will honor their work, and that he will help them honor him with their work.

3. Honoring God's provision

Main Point: Honoring God for all that he provides.

Veterans Day and a number of other occasions honor men and women who fought in America's wars. As Christians, we can certainly honor those who've served our country to preserve our freedoms. At the same time, we can honor God for all that he provides every day.

Occasions to use: Veterans Day; Memorial Day; anytime

Scripture: "Love must be sincere. Hate what is evil; cling to what is good. Be devoted to one another in brotherly love. Honor one another above yourselves" (Romans 12:9-10).

Quote: "Courage is almost a contradiction in terms. It means a strong desire to live taking the form of readiness to die."—G.K. Chesterton

Hymn: "God of Our Fathers, Whose Almighty Hand"

Contemporary Chorus: "All the Honor and Praise"

Take-away: Distribute small Christian flags as worshippers leave your building. One online source for these is www.flags-wholesale.com.

4. Honoring the family of God

Main Point: Honor the institution of the family and the institution of the church—God's family.

Strong families make for strong churches and strong communities. God created the family, and he extends the idea of family as an illustration of the church. Part of being the family of God is supporting each other just as an actual family would support its members.

Occasions to use: Mother's Day; Father's Day; National Family Week; Christmas holiday season

Scripture: "As we have opportunity, let us do good to all people, especially to those who belong to the family of believers" (Galatians 6:10).

Quote: "A man ought to live so that everybody knows he is a Christian… and most of all, his family ought to know."—Dwight L. Moody

Hymn: "Children of the Heavenly Father"

Contemporary Chorus: "God Is in the House"

Take-away: Recruit people with digital cameras to take photos of family groups after the service. In addition to e-mailing the photos to the families in your church, create a bulletin board with the heading "Family of God" and prints of the photos; you can also put your photos on the church's Web site.

4 Looks at God's Character

1. Comfort and remembrance

Main Point: During tough times, we can be certain that God watches over and protects us.

Everyone is touched by grief and tragedy at some point in life. It's especially disturbing when a tragedy occurs unexpectedly. Such times can leave people feeling insecure and in danger. Spend time remembering those affected by grief or tragedy, but also focusing on God's ultimate protection and promised victory.

Occasions to use: After a beloved member of the church dies; following a local accident or tragedy; anniversary of September 11

Scripture: "The Lord will keep you from all harm—he will watch over your life; the Lord will watch over your coming and going both now and forevermore" (Psalm 121:7-8).

Quote: "The ultimate measure of a man is not where he stands in moments of comfort and convenience, but where he stands at times of challenge and controversy."—Martin Luther King Jr.

Hymn: "Like a River Glorious"

Contemporary Chorus: "Lord, Lift Me Up"

Take-away: Give each worshipper a candle to remind them that Jesus is the light of the world. No matter how hopeless things seem, nothing can shake the foundation of that truth!

2. Jewish holidays

Main Point: While Christians don't typically observe Jewish celebrations, these holidays offer the promise of forgiveness and new beginnings.

Rosh Hashana is a good example of a Jewish holy day. Commonly known as the Jewish new year, it celebrates the creation of the world and provides a time for reflection and self-evaluation. Yom Kippur, the Day of Atonement, begins 10 days after the Jewish New Year and marks a new beginning when God forgives us and we forgive each other.

Occasions to use: Find the dates of a dozen Jewish holidays at the Judaism 101 Web site (www.jewfaq.org). For example, Rosh Hashana occurs in September or early October.

Scripture: "If anyone is in Christ, he is a new creation; the old has gone, the new has come! All this is from God, who reconciled us to himself through Christ" (2 Corinthians 5:17-18).

Quote: "Reflect upon your present blessings, of which every man
has many, not on your past misfortunes, of which all men have
some."—Charles Dickens

Hymn: "Jesus, I Come"

Contemporary Chorus: "New Creation"

Take-away: Give each worshipper a pad of Post-it notes. Encourage
people to write a blessing from God on each page of the pad, and
place the pages around their homes to reflect on them often.

3. God's Word

Main Point: God personally communicates with us.

Help members of your church focus on the practical guidance God
gives us in Scripture—his way of speaking clearly to each of us.

Occasions to use: Anytime

Scripture: "All Scripture is God-breathed and is useful for teaching, rebuking,
correcting and training in righteousness, so that the man of God may
be thoroughly equipped for every good work" (2 Timothy 3:16-17).

Quote: "Think like a wise man but communicate in the language of the
people."—William Butler Yeats

Hymn: "Wonderful Words of Life"

Contemporary Chorus: "Word of God Speak"

Take-away: Distribute a portion of an easy-to-read rendering of God's
Word, such as *The Message of Hope* (NavPress, 2001).

4. God is with us!

Main Point: Help your church focus on Jesus: Immanuel—God with us.

Whether it's Christmas or any other time of the year, celebrate the
gift of Christ, who humbled himself, came to earth, ministered among
people, and accepted the penalty of death so we don't have to.

Occasions to use: Sundays during the Christmas season; anytime

Scripture: "The angel answered, 'The Holy Spirit will come upon you,
and the power of the Most High will overshadow you. So the holy
one to be born will be called the Son of God' " (Luke 1:35).

Quote: "How many observe Christ's birthday! How few, his precepts! O! 'tis
easier to keep Holidays than Commandments."—Benjamin Franklin

Hymn: "Come, Thou Long-Expected Jesus"

Contemporary Chorus: "Rejoice (A Christmas Song)"

Take-away: No matter what time of year it is, give a gold Christmas
ornament to each worshipper as he or she exits the service. The
Magi's gift of gold (Matthew 2:11) represented an acknowledg-
ment that Jesus is truly the Son of God.

3 Services of Reflection and Inspiration

1. Gratitude

Main Point: Gratefulness to God

Most people know that what we now call the Thanksgiving holiday was first observed by the Pilgrims and Indians to celebrate a bountiful harvest. However, many of us forget that the Pilgrims came to the New World to seek religious freedom. Whether during the Thanksgiving holiday—or at any time—you can fill your service with a sense of gratefulness to God for the privilege of worshipping him freely.

Occasions to use: Thanksgiving weekend; anytime

Scripture: "Let the word of Christ dwell in you richly as you teach and admonish one another with all wisdom, and as you sing psalms, hymns and spiritual songs with gratitude in your hearts to God" (Colossians 3:16).

Quote: "True thanksgiving means that we need to thank God for what He has done for us, and not to tell Him what we have done for him."—George R. Hendrick

Hymn: "Now Thank We All Our God"

Contemporary Chorus: "Better Than Life"

Take-away: Purchase boxes of thank-you notes and distribute one to each member of your congregation. Encourage each person to write a quick thank-you note to God for a recent blessing, then to place the card in the envelope and seal it. Finally, each person should address the envelope to himself or herself. They should tuck the cards in their Bibles and open them sometime in the future when they're feeling low—as a reminder to be thankful for all that God provides.

2. Uniquely made

Main Point: Celebration of God's creation of each person.

God doesn't simply stamp out carbon copies. Each person is unique—even identical twins aren't completely alike! Although they have identical DNA, their fingerprints are different! Isn't it strange that the world can accept that each person has unique fingerprints, yet has such a difficult time admitting that it takes a Creator to come up with each unique design.

Occasions to use: National Sanctity of Human Life Day; anytime

Scripture: "You created my inmost being; you knit me together in my mother's womb. I praise you because I am fearfully and wonderfully made" (Psalm 139:13-14).

Quote: "You are one of a kind. The world will never see anyone like you again. You have unique perceptions and your own contribution to make."—Barbara Sher

Hymn: "All Creatures of Our God and King"

Contemporary Chorus: "I Will Sing"

Take-away: Distribute note cards to members of the congregation. Encourage people to read all of Psalm 139 at home, and then note on their card all the ways God makes them unique, then thanking him for each way.

3. Humility

Main Point: Perhaps no single word describes what the attitude of Christians should be as fully as humility.

While the world says, "aim for fame," Christians serve tirelessly in thankless ministry. While the world shouts, "show me the money," Christians give. While the world urges, "strive for success," Christians simply ask God where he wants to use them. While the world whispers, "seize power," Christians willingly surrender to God's will. These are the marks of humility.

Occasions to use: Anytime

Scripture: "The greatest among you will be your servant. For whoever exalts himself will be humbled, and whoever humbles himself will be exalted" (Matthew 23:11-12).

Quote: "I believe that the first test of a truly great man is his humility… Really great men have a curious feeling that the greatness is not of them, but through them. And they see something divine in every other man and are endlessly, foolishly, incredibly merciful."—John Ruskin

Hymn: "Not I but Christ"

Contemporary Chorus: "Deeper"

Take-away: Lance Armstrong made wearing bracelets cool. For less than $1 each (one source is www.abetteridea.com), you can have bracelets custom-made. Emboss them with the simple word "Humility," or screenprint the phrase "Whoever humbles himself will be exalted."

Recharging Your Personal and Family Life

T he whole idea of caring for yourself and your family is quite plain
and utterly simple: If you don't take time away from ministry to
focus on your personal needs, neither your personal and family
life nor your ministry will be effective. You're one person and you live one
complete life. You can't simply remove one part of your life and ignore
it. Instead, you need to aim for balance among the various areas of your
life—including managing your time, maintaining your spiritual health, and
deepening relationships with your family. The following ideas will help you
move closer to that place of balance.

Section 5: Table of Contents

12 Quick Spiritual Boosters

Even if you're taking care of your body and stimulating your mind, chances are good that you'll continue to feel out of sorts if you're neglecting your spiritual health. Whenever you're feeling like a deflated balloon spiritually, try one or more of these activities to inflate your spirits.

1. Page through your church directory

When you're wondering if your ministry is worth all the frustrations and disappointments, prayerfully and thankfully meditate through your church directory. As you look through the directory name by name, picture the face of each individual. Ponder the growth in each person's life. Reflect on any life-changing decisions that person has made over the years. Remind yourself that sometimes it takes years to see rewards—a solid lay leader who was once a hesitant visitor, a fun and amazing Sunday school teacher who used to hide behind the curriculum book.

Paging through the directory also helps you realize how blessed you are. How could one person have so many friends? Think back on the memories of camping trips, softball games, banquets, weddings, births, children's programs, and so on. Even difficult memories will be meaningful—counseling a troubled family, conducting funerals, visiting emergency rooms, praying for rebellious children. Deep friendships are forged in difficult times. Realize how blessed you are to serve in ministry at your church.

2. Spiritual reading

Set aside time to read—15 minutes a day, one hour a week, one day a month, one week a year. Schedule these pockets ahead of time and protect your schedule. Choose spiritual-formation material to read through, or tackle those classics of church history. Don't say that you don't have time to read. In 15 minutes a day, by reading just 200 words a minute, you can plow through more than a million words a year. Aim high.

3. Take a prayer retreat

Spend a whole day in prayer. First, pray through the attributes and character of God. Be impressed again with who God is. Then pray for yourself, confessing your sins. Ask for God to give you strength and to equip you for meeting the challenges of ministry. Recommit yourself to be faithful. Pray for your marriage and your family. Pray for your church, each ministry and colleague. Pray for individuals in your church, bringing their needs before the Lord. Ask God to provide insight for ministering to them; share with God your vision for each person's potential. Pray for missionaries you and your church support. Pray for other pastors and their ministries.

CROSS REFERENCE:
See also "2 Self-Directed Retreats" later in this section, page 112.

4. Conduct a reading fast

You can get so caught up in reading books that you neglect The Book. The cure: Read only the Scriptures for several days, or even a month. Don't read books, newspapers, magazines, or even browse the Internet. At first it will seem difficult, but it will become an exciting adventure you'll always remember. Amazingly, the entire Bible takes about 80 hours to read out loud. You can read the New Testament in less than 20 hours. Set a goal, and fall in love with the Word all over again.

5. Study one book of the Bible

For a month, or even longer, study only one book of the Bible. Read it through many times. Read it in as many different translations as you can. Work through the language, syntax, and vocabulary. Outline it. Read commentaries. Develop a notebook of material as you gain a level of mastery of the book.

6. Study one subject

Study a single biblical subject—one as broad as music or as narrow as the Urim and Thummim. Trace the subject through biblical history. Do the Old and New Testaments differ on the topic? How is it relevant for today?

7. Practice solitude

Take time to be alone with God. Take care to choose a place where you won't be distracted by people or things to do. Search online for ministry retreat centers or camps that offer pastors reduced-cost or free accommodations. Or check into a hotel for 24 hours. Just be alone with God for a whole day.

8. Spend time in a crowd

When Jesus saw the multitudes, he was moved with compassion. Go to a place where you can observe people. Allow yourself to be burdened with the great needs of our culture. Pray for the people you see. Thank God for the ways he uses you to make a difference in people's lives.

9. Get up early

Few things are as precious as the solitude of an early morning. The world remains asleep, but you're awake and spending time with God. You haven't uncovered the problems of the day, so your mind is less cluttered with distractions. Of course, spending an early morning with God starts the night before—get to bed on time.

10. Stay up late

Just as the early morning is quiet, the late night can be a time of solitude. However, you'll face more obstacles to spending time with God at night. You'll need to put aside the problems of the day and avoid distractions like the TV.

11. Memorize and meditate

Take time to memorize Scripture. Find a method that works for you. To avoid simply memorizing words without meaning, meditate on the verse or passage first. Reflect on the passage from different angles. Emphasize different words and reflect how focusing on different words changes the perspective. Ask the who, what, where, when, why, and how questions. Apply the passage by thinking about how your life or faith would be different without the truth of this specific Scripture.

12. Listen to a message

Listen to someone else preach. Fully engage in what the speaker is saying. Take notes and look up the Scripture references. Allow yourself to be fed. Many Internet sites post messages you can listen to. Some sites also include recordings of great preachers of the past.

16 Prayer Ideas for When You Don't Have Time to Pray

For many Christians, including pastors, spending time in prayer can be tough. How are you supposed to pray when you're too tired, too drained, or just don't feel like it? These suggestions can help no matter how stressed or crowded your life feels.

1. During down time

Ask the Spirit of God to remind you to pray when you're in line at the supermarket, waiting in a doctor's office, or stopped in traffic. Even if you don't have much time, simply lift the thoughts on your heart to God. Pray for people by name, even if you don't know what specific needs they have. God will work even if you simply ask his blessing on them.

2. While you walk

While you're walking to an appointment inside a building, pray for the people you're going to see. On the elevator ride to the appropriate floor, pray for the people on the elevator and others God reminds you of. Concentrate on specific requests for specific people, including your family and yourself.

3. When you're driving

Pray whether you're stopped at red lights or cruising along the freeway. Think about how much time you spend in your car on errands and visits. Instead of being frustrated by traffic, you can log many hours offering praises and requests to God.

4. While you're falling asleep

As your mind wanders, focus your brain on a few simple prayers. Pray about a specific area of your life and ministry each night: Monday—worship services; Tuesday—your sermon; Wednesday—Sunday school classes. And so on.

5. About something new

It's easy to repeat the same prayers over and over. Instead, direct yourself to pray about different subjects as God brings them to mind. For example, in the morning pray for other churches and their pastors. In the afternoon, pray for Christian authors and speakers. In the early evening, pray for people in the media—actors, news anchors, directors, and producers. In the late evening, pray for leaders in government.

6. Through the week

Each week you can pray for various groups in our society. On Mondays, pray for governments and countries. On Tuesdays, pray about the United States, the president and cabinet, senators, congressman, and governors. On Wednesdays, pray for people you knew growing up. On Thursdays, focus your prayers on past communities and churches you served. By sticking to a prayer plan, you'll be more motivated to pray, and by rotating your prayers, they'll remain fresh.

7. Through Scripture

Turn to specific Scripture passages and pray that on behalf of family members, yourself, or your church. Some of Paul's prayers in the epistles are spiritual dynamite. Read or even memorize passages like Philippians 1:9-11; Colossians 1:9-12; Ephesians 1:15-21; and Ephesians 3:16-21, using them as templates for prayer for different ministries in your church. They'll provide real concerns to speak with God about.

8. About truths in Scripture

Rather than specific passages, think about holiness, for example, and pray throughout the day for God to work in different people to make them grow in holiness. Choose a new issue each day of the week. Pray through the fruit of the Spirit for individuals in your life, choosing one day to pray on the subject of love, praying the next day on joy, and after that, praying a day for peace, patience, kindness, and so on. In time, you'll have prayed for God to develop these qualities in many people's lives.

9. As you talk to people

When people ask you to pray for them, send up a "thought prayer" while the person is talking to you. Of course, you can pray for the request again when God brings it to mind. But one prayer is all God needs to move into action in someone's life.

10. For a few seconds

While it's good to keep a regular time of prayer in your life—in the morning, or at lunchtime, or in the evening—it's also great to pray for a few seconds at a time whenever a need or concern comes to mind. God hears and answers even our most spontaneous and simple prayers.

11. Anytime God nudges you

For example, if you're at a church meeting and the Spirit suddenly whispers, "Pray for [name]," pray right then. Don't hesitate. Make it a habit to pray when you sense God urging you to.

12. With a core group

Once a week, get together with some trusted fellow pastors, leaders of your church, or members of your small group. As you pray openly and honestly, the camaraderie you develop will be a great encouragement for your prayer life.

13. With your church staff

No reason to be too elaborate or formal. Just get together in a room, stand, and encourage each person to share one prayer request for that week. Pray for the person to your right, or left, or whatever. This not only draws your staff together, but makes them aware of your commitment to prayer.

14. With your spouse

Choose a time when you'll both be home—before bedtime, in the morning at breakfast, or before meals. Bonus: Both of you will develop a more committed prayer life.

15. With your children

Praying at bedtime alone with each child often works best. Ask what's on your child's heart, and pray specifically about that issue.

16. On trips and family outings

Make it a habit and part of the fabric of your family life to pray before you start the car. Even if your kids groan about it, they'll appreciate and remember it.

2 Self-Directed Retreats

Taking time away to be with God is essential, especially for pastors who experience continual pressure to be spiritual giants. Personal retreats provide a great opportunity for a spiritual tuneup—a chance to be real with God, to identify areas that need growth, and to celebrate your relationship with him.

Self-directed retreats can be as short as a few hours at a park with your Bible or as long as a full weekend on a camp out or at a hotel. These retreats each contain three one-hour sessions. If you're doing a half-day retreat, simply proceed directly through all three sessions. If your retreat will be longer, plan other activities (such as walks, reading, napping) and times of worship and prayer between the three sessions.

Retreat 1. Practicing God's Presence

Supplies:
A Bible, a journal, a pen, a small spiral notebook, a photocopy of this retreat guide, and a project to work on (such as woodworking, a painting or drawing, a photo album, a tent to set up, tools to tune up the car, needlework, handicrafts, a model car to construct, or any project that requires you to use your hands)

Session 1

(10 minutes)

This retreat will focus on clearing your mind and heart of worries, concerns, and other thoughts in order to focus specifically on God's presence. Of course, distracting thoughts will want to creep in. So grab your spiral notebook and begin the retreat by listing every worry, concern, situation, or nitpicky detail about home or church that might distract your thoughts. When you're done, pray about every item on the list. Surrender each one into God's hands, committing to address it when you return. Ask God's help to mentally set aside these concerns during your retreat.

Keep this notebook with you during the retreat. If new distracting thoughts interrupt your focus on God, write them down and set the notebook aside. This relieves the worry of forgetting something important—when you return from the retreat, you can resume dealing with these issues.

(25 minutes)

Now, read through the following accounts of the ways God's people have experienced his presence.
- Moses (Exodus 3:1-15; 14:1-31)
- Gideon (Judges 6:11-39)
- Samuel (1 Samuel 2:21)
- Elijah (1 Kings 19:3-13)
- Mary of Bethany (Luke 10:38-42)
- The early church (Acts 2:1-4; 8:26-40; 13:1-3)
- Paul (Acts 9:1-22; 2 Corinthians 12:1-10)

Some of these people experienced God's presence in miraculous ways, while others experienced his presence in less dramatic ways. Take some time to think about these questions:
- Which story do you relate to most?
- Which best represents the way you experience God's presence?

Retreat 1. Practicing God's Presence

(25 minutes)

Use your journal to write a brief spiritual autobiography. Reflect on your own personal experience of God's presence. Use these questions to guide your writing:

- How did you experience God's presence when you were younger?
- How have you experienced God's presence in recent years?
- When have you felt distant from God, unable to sense his presence?
- Have you experienced God's presence in a dramatic, emotional, or "miraculous" way? If so, when?
- How have you experienced God's presence in less dramatic, everyday ways?

Session 2

(20 minutes)

Take out your spiral notebook and draw seven columns, labeling each for a day of the week. Along the left side, list the hours of the day, beginning with the time you normally wake up and ending when you normally sleep. Now do your best to note your daily habits and routines in each column—what is your ordinary life like? Think of specifics, filling each hour of each day with a short description of your actions.

Once you've written a thorough description of your daily life, evaluate it using these questions:

- When in your daily routine do you feel closest to God? Put a star by the times or days when you feel you experience God's presence the most.
- When in your routine do you feel farthest from God? Or when are your thoughts most distracted from God's presence? Put a circle by the times or days you've chosen.

Now look at the items you've marked. What does this tell you about your own understanding of what it means to experience God's presence? What insights does this give you about your spiritual practices?

(20 minutes)

Brother Lawrence, a monk in the 1600s, believed that we experience God's presence during our regular, day-to-day employments and routines. He felt closest to God when doing the ordinary, routine, mundane work of his everyday life as a worker in the kitchen at his monastery. In his book *The Practice of the Presence of God,* he stated his belief that Christians don't need to separate "prayer time" from everyday life—that each regular moment of every ordinary day is a time for communion with God.

Retreat 1. Practicing God's Presence

Look again at the notes you've written describing your own daily routines. Are there areas of your everyday life where you could incorporate this mind-set? Reread each item on your list and consider the question: "How could this be an opportunity for me to experience God's presence?"

(20 minutes)

Brother Lawrence described his practice of God's presence as "an habitual, silent, and secret conversation of the soul with God…My most usual method is this simple attention, and such a general passionate regard to God…If sometimes my thoughts wander from it by necessity or infirmity, I am presently recalled by inward motions."

Brother Lawrence's teachings about how other Christians can develop this same connection with God can be summarized as follows:

First, we must recognize that we already have God's presence continually with us. We must begin the discipline of constantly reminding ourselves of God's presence in our lives and focusing on this truth, choosing not to lose our awareness of this truth when we are distracted by worries and concerns. In other words, though our minds will at times be occupied with work, our hearts need to remain focused on God. As Christians, we must use our wills and determination to retain a continual awareness of God's presence. As we work on developing this habit, we gain the ability to see God's presence everywhere and to experience what it means to "pray continually" (1 Thessalonians 5:17).

Take some time to think and pray about Brother Lawrence's teachings, reflecting on these questions:

- What is your reaction to Brother Lawrence's teachings?
- How often are you focused on God's presence despite the other work or concerns of your daily life?
- Practically speaking, how could you develop a greater attention to God's presence?
- What challenges do you face in the 21st century that didn't affect a monk in the 17th century? How can you overcome these challenges to put these principles into action?

Retreat 1. Practicing God's Presence

Session 3
(45 minutes)

Take 45 minutes (or longer) to work on a project you've brought with you. During the entire time period, focus on God's presence and be attentive to his communication with you. You can speak out loud or sit in silence. Just enjoy being with God as you work. If distractions pop into your mind, simply write them down in your notebook and set it aside.

(15 minutes)

Read the following Psalms:
- Psalm 16:11
- Psalm 31:19-20
- Psalm 84:1-4, 10-12
- Psalm 89:15-16
- Psalm 139:1-18

In your journal, write a description of your experience of God's presence while you did your project. Answering these questions can help you get started:
- How did you feel as you were focused on God's presence?
- What is God like?

Praise God for who he is, and ask for his help in your efforts to develop a habit of practicing his presence in your daily life.

Retreat 2. Healing From Criticism

Supplies:

A Bible, a journal, a pen, a photocopy of this retreat guide, one plain white T-shirt, permanent markers, a hand mirror, scissors, your favorite shirt, blank paper, an envelope, and a stamp

Session 1

(15 minutes)

As a pastor, you face criticism. People in your congregation constantly evaluate your "performance," critique your personality, and put pressure on you to be "perfect." In addition, Satan attacks you in every way he can to injure you, damage your family, and incapacitate your ministry.

Read the following Scriptures and consider how they relate to your own experience as a pastor:

- Psalm 3:1-6
- Psalm 35:10-16
- Psalm 56:1-4
- Psalm 109:1-5
- 1 Corinthians 4:10-13
- 1 Peter 5:6-11

Now read this paraphrase of Psalm 56:1-2 from *The Message:* "Take my side, God—I'm getting kicked around, stomped on every day. Not a day goes by but somebody beats me up." Have you felt this way as a pastor? Can you relate to the emotions conveyed in these psalms? Which one do you relate to best? When have you felt "attacked" by others?

(25 minutes)

Think about specific criticism you've had to face as a pastor. Take some time to journal your responses to these questions:

- How have you been labeled, unfairly judged, or gossiped about?
- What baggage are you carrying because of conflicts with difficult people?
- How do you respond to criticism?
- How does it feel to be criticized and continually evaluated?
- How has the burden of criticism and pressure affected your spiritual or emotional health?
- What internal injuries do you have as a result of insensitive comments or the constant pressure to be perfect?

Retreat 2. Healing From Criticism

(10 minutes)

Now it's time to name those specific criticisms, difficult situations, hurts, frustrations, grudges, disappointments, pressures, and judgments made against you as a pastor. Take a marker and write on the white T-shirt a word or phrase to describe every situation you think of. Do your best to completely cover the T-shirt. When you're done, put on the T-shirt.

(10 minutes)

Take time to pray, speaking honestly with God about how it feels to wear the burdens and baggage represented on the T-shirt. Like the psalmists, talk to God candidly about your feelings regarding the situations you've written. When you're done praying, keep the shirt on until you do Session 2. (If necessary, you can wear something over the T-shirt so others don't see what you've written.)

Session 2

(10 minutes)

Use the hand mirror to look at yourself wearing the T-shirt. Spend time evaluating how wearing the T-shirt reflects your experience of the labels, judgments, and frustrations you "wear" on a daily basis.

(30 minutes)

Read Psalm 109:21-22. In your journal, reflect in writing how the various criticisms and tough situations represented on your T-shirt have affected you. Use these questions as you write:
- How do the situations on the T-shirt affect the way you lead?
- How do they change the way you relate to your family?
- How do they influence the way you relate to challenging people?
- How do they affect the way you view yourself?
- How do they shape the way you relate to God?

(20 minutes)

Read Psalm 147:3. Take off the T-shirt and study the words written on it again. As a prayer exercise, use scissors to cut up the T-shirt into small pieces. Each time you cut through a word or phrase, ask God to help you forgive those involved and to remove that burden from your life. When you're done praying, throw the remnants of the T-shirt away (or burn them in a campfire).

Retreat 2. Healing From Criticism

Session 3

(15 minutes)

Now that you've symbolically removed and destroyed the baggage of criticism and pressure, look at the *real you* in the hand mirror as you read and reflect on these passages:

- Psalm 139:1-18
- 1 Corinthians 1:4-9
- Ephesians 1:3-12
- Ephesians 2:4-10

Now pray, reflecting on these passages and what they affirm about how God views you and how he equips you to fulfill your calling as a pastor.

(15 minutes)

Put on your favorite shirt to replace the shirt of burdens and baggage. Read the following passages aloud, reminding yourself of what God wants you to put on and "wear" instead of criticism and labels. After you've read all the passages aloud, take some time to pray and reflect on what they mean to you.

- Romans 13:11-14
- Galatians 3:26-27
- Ephesians 4:22-24
- Ephesians 6:10-18
- Colossians 3:12-17
- 1 Thessalonians 5:8-11

(20 minutes)

Select one of the passages listed above and write it out using your own words. Then take some time to complete the following thoughts on your paper:

- God has made me unique, with many gifts and talents, such as…
- God has called me to the ministry and has equipped me with these spiritual gifts and personal strengths…
- God has used me in many ways to influence my congregation and community, such as…
- God is helping me grow in the following areas…

When you're done, fold up your papers and put them in an envelope. Seal the envelope, stamp it, and address it to yourself. After your retreat, give the envelope to a trusted and responsible friend, asking that person to leave it sealed and drop it in the mail for you in about a month. When you receive it, read it again as a reminder of God's love for you and his calling on your life.

■ ■ ■

Retreat 2. Healing From Criticism

(10 minutes)

Conclude your retreat by singing (or reading aloud) the words of this hymn. Each time you mention a part of your body, touch it with your hands or lift it up to God as a physical symbol of your renewed commitment to serve him fully, despite criticism and pressures you face.

"Take My Life and Let It Be" by Frances R. Havergal

Take my life, and let it be consecrated, Lord, to Thee.
Take my moments and my days; let them flow in ceaseless praise.
Take my hands, and let them move at the impulse of Thy love.
Take my feet, and let them be swift and beautiful for Thee.

Take my voice, and let me sing always, only, for my King.
Take my lips, and let them be filled with messages from Thee.
Take my silver and my gold; not a mite would I withhold.
Take my intellect, and use every power as Thou shalt choose.

Take my will, and make it Thine; it shall be no longer mine.
Take my heart, it is Thine own; it shall be Thy royal throne.
Take my love, my Lord, I pour at Thy feet its treasure store.
Take myself, and I will be ever, only, all for Thee.

31 Creative Ways to Spend Time With Your Spouse

If you're married, you've probably already realized that your spouse is your biggest and best fan, cheerleader, coach, and player—sometimes all rolled into one! But with the crazy life of a pastor and a pastor's household, you also realize that unless you truly work at growing your relationship, your once-thriving marriage can easily become a stale institution (or perhaps worse, just a mere convenience). The following ideas focus on adding a bit of fun, a hint of romance, and a good dose of quality time to your marriage.

1. Do housework together

Neither of you really wants to do it, so put on some fun, energetic music and work on the same chores together (instead of doing separate chores at the same time). Afterward, clean up and go out for a shake or piece of pie.

2. Connect in a crowd

Hang out near each other in the after-church services, at parties, or any time you're in a gathering. Being together in conversations with others helps you connect to each other.

3. Read the Song of Solomon to each other

Be serious or melodramatic or passionate. Act it out if you want!

4. Travel together

People in ministry often have speaking engagements. Go with your spouse when he or she speaks at a meeting, and be a silent cheerleader (and prayer supporter).

5. Step outside your comfort zone

Attend an event or participate in an activity that your spouse likes to do even if you have no interest in it. For example, maybe your spouse likes baseball. Go to a game together.

6. Listen to music

Take a relaxing drive with the volume turned up, or drive to a park and sit with a battery operated CD player. Each of you should bring a CD of your favorite music.

7. Taste-test different places

Have lunch at a deli, a sandwich shop, a Chinese restaurant, or a coffee shop. Or choose a coffee-shop chain you both like and make a trip to different outlets in different parts of the city each week.

8. Go on a mission trip

Spend a few hours working together at a local soup kitchen, a day working on a Habitat for Humanity home, or a longer trip with the youth group.

9. Laugh together

Simply share a couple of jokes, watch a funny movie, or pop in a DVD of a comedian you both like. Or go to dinner with another couple who share your sense of humor.

10. Celebrate "point" anniversaries

Don't just celebrate your marriage on your anniversary date. Once in a while, celebrate when you've been married 7.6 years or another crazy and unexpected time.

11. Celebrate other anniversaries

Besides your wedding anniversary, celebrate the anniversary of your first kiss, your first date, your first fight, the first time you ate at your favorite restaurant together. Be fun and creative. Compile a list of your firsts and use any excuse to celebrate them together.

12. Share a sunset cup of coffee

If you're both home, head out to your deck, porch, or yard. Or drag lawn chairs and a thermos of coffee to church and catch your spouse for a quick cup on the church lawn before the next meeting.

13. Experiment with kissing in different locations

Corner your spouse on an elevator (when you're alone—don't be an exhibitionist) or in the church kitchen. Pucker up in the middle of some pine trees. Buss in a bus station. Some marriage experts say the first sign of romance tapering off is when couples stop kissing. So keep at it and see what locales you like the best.

14. Go to a gallery

After you spend time enjoying art together, take some paints, colored pencils, or molding clay, and try to re-create your favorite piece. Share with each other why you chose that particular piece of artwork and have a laugh over your re-created versions.

15. Go to a concert

Surprise your spouse by buying tickets when a favorite performer comes to town. Go all out to make it a special evening. That evening or the next day, surprise your spouse with the CD by the performer. You'll both remember the special night every time you hear the CD.

16. Bake brownies or cookies

Nothin' says lovin' like somethin' from the oven! If you're making cookies, use fun cookie cutters and enjoy decorating them together.

17. Visit a state park or nature center

Purposely set out to use your senses (sight, smell, sound, taste, touch) as much as possible. Point out sense-provoking things to each other—even make a list if you want.

18. Create a culinary rendezvous at church

If your spouse is too busy to get away from church for lunch, find an out-of-the-way room, pull in a card table, cover it with a fancy tablecloth, and set the table with your best china, silver, and candlesticks. Put some romantic music on a portable CD player, and lay out a feast—even if it's McDonald's or Subway.

19. Sit at a lake

If you unexpectedly find yourselves free for a couple of hours on a nice day, throw some lawn chairs and a loaf of bread in your car and head off to feed the ducks or geese while you chat.

20. Veg out in front of the TV

When you see your spouse watching a favorite show, or just chilling, join in. Don't think of it as a waste of time to sit in front of the TV. Instead, look at it as a good use of time for just vegging with your spouse. And don't keep your hands to yourself. Pamper each other with a backrub or footrub.

21. Accompany your spouse on mundane chores

If you must, you can squeeze in some work productivity—make phone calls while your spouse stops at the post office, or jot down sermon notes while your spouse runs into the store.

22. Have lunch at home once a week

Change your routine to have lunch with your spouse at least once a week. Or if you'd rather have a romantic rendezvous once in a while, go for it!

23. Take the day off work on your spouse's birthday

Plan a day trip your spouse will enjoy. Or just head to a favorite coffee shop to play board games or chat.

24. Go away at home

Is there somewhere your spouse has always wanted to visit? For a surprise, decorate part of your house or yard to resemble that location, create a meal, play the native music, and even dress in the style of that area. Together, watch a video about this place from the library, and browse through a travel guide you picked up at your local bookstore.

25. Go to a library or bookstore together

Do either of you have some reading or studying to do? You can both study. Or if your spouse needs to study and you don't, find a subject to study—like plants, home improvement, or how coffee plantations grow beans. If you're at a bookstore with a cafe, have a cup of coffee and dessert together.

26. Takin' a ride

Get away from it all. Hop in the car (or motorcycle!) and just head out on the highway. Blow the gas budget once in a while on a long and relaxing ride with the windows down. Don't determine a destination beforehand—find one together!

27. Grocery shop

Split up the list and head separate directions so you can get the shopping done quickly. For the fun of it, each of you can choose a surprise food (like oxtails or a can of coconut syrup) that you can try together.

28. Plant a garden

Make it your special time to tend the garden together. If neither of you has a green thumb, visit an orchard to pick fruit together.

29. Volunteer at a community event

As a couple, work at a booth during a local festival, or volunteer to help at your kids' school carnival.

30. Light up your night

Create special lighting in your bedroom—string Christmas lights around your bed, plug in the old lava lamp, or light as many candles as you can find. Cuddle up with a cup of hot cocoa and talk about what first attracted you to each other. Be romantic.

31. Don't fly—drive

If you're going to a conference or another event, drive instead of flying. During the hours on the road, you'll find yourselves making interesting conversation.

10 Awesome Things to Do With Your Kids

You know that spending time with each of your children is critical for building your relationships. But sometimes you struggle to find an activity to do together. When you're tired and lacking creativity, try one of the following ideas. Or use the list to get your own creative juices flowing.

1. Celebrate a rite of passage

When your child turns 13, take him or her on a special overnight trip for just the two of you. Do something fun together. Tell your new teen what you envision for his or her life. Be sure to focus on the positive. Present him or her with a token of this significant time in life—perhaps a cross necklace, a purity ring, a teen study Bible, or some other valuable and lasting memento. Pray a special prayer of blessing for your child. And be sure to express your love, even if your teen doesn't seem to want to hear it.

2. Make a date with each child once a month

Take your child out to lunch with no agenda in mind. Talk about whatever's on your child's heart. This can be an especially important time to connect with teenagers. Younger children will also enjoy this special time alone when they don't have to share Mom or Dad with anyone else. No matter what their ages, this one-on-one time tells your children that they're valuable and worth spending your time with them. Mix in some fun dates as well—mini-golfing, seeing a movie, or blowing a few bucks at an arcade.

3. Relive the past

If your kids are interested in family history, go through old photo albums and tell stories about the people in the pictures. They'll especially like seeing pictures of you growing up. Share memories from your childhood. For a special memento, write down memories, stories, and facts from the years when you were growing up (hobbies, favorites, and so on) for each child. This will become more and more meaningful as your kids get older.

4. Play your child's favorite video game

Will you be terrible at it? Probably. Will your child love the fact that he or she is beating Mom or Dad? Yes! Will it be meaningful to your child that you took an interest in something that you're probably not crazy about? Absolutely.

5. Connect with your family daily

Try to take at least a half hour every day to reconnect with each child, focusing solely on him or her. Turn off the TV and computer, or at least go into another room where you won't be tempted to "just take a peek" at e-mail. Look your child in the eye, talk, and play together.

6. Learn from your child

Ask each child to give you a basic overview of something he or she really enjoys. Ask your son to show you the basics of skateboarding jumps. Ask your daughter to show you the basic moves from her dance class. The point isn't for you to learn how to do these things yourself, but to have a better understanding of your child's interest when he or she talks to you about it.

7. Celebrate!

Make a list of special but out-of-the-ordinary reasons to celebrate with each child. Think beyond birthdays and anniversaries. Have a "birthday" party on the anniversary date that your child made a commitment to Jesus. Serve a favorite dinner for a child who brings home a hard-earned A on a test or paper.

8. Read a book with each child

Choose a classic such as *The Lion, the Witch and the Wardrobe; The Secret Garden;* or another tale that's stood the test of time. Read a few pages a night with each child. When your child has learned to read, have him or her read aloud to you.

9. Go geocaching

This modern game is a hunt for a hidden object using a global positioning system (GPS) unit. People hide caches all over the world, with the locations listed on the Internet. The game involves using a GPS unit to find the hidden "treasure." When you and your kids find it, leave something there for the next hunters to find. Go to www.geocaching.com for all the details.

10. Make memory boxes together

At the end of the school year, gather a bunch of craft supplies. Help your child decorate a box for the previous school year. Label the box with the child's name, age, grade, teacher, and school. Then, go through the stack of school papers, science projects, art projects, and report cards collected throughout the year. Decide together on the most important pieces to keep. While you work, reminisce about all that happened over the previous year. Focus on positive values and character traits your child is developing.

23 Fun and Simple Family Getaways and Events

Need to get away with your whole family, but you don't have much time or a lot of cash? The following activities are all free, or at least relatively inexpensive, and can be done in a few hours or less. As you have fun together, watch your relationships deepen and grow.

Classic Kids' Favorites!

1. Water world

Grab your swimsuits and sunscreen and spend the day with your kids at a water park.

2. See (but don't feed) the animals

Check out God's amazing creativity with a family trip to the zoo or an aquarium.

3. See a flick

Head out to a movie you've all wanted to see. Or go to an IMAX movie, and then talk together about what you learned in the film.

4. Team spirit

Grab the face paint and pompons, and then cheer on a local team as a family at a sporting event.

5. Discover your inner child

Take a trip to a children's museum and explore the exhibits while playing with your kids.

On-Location Fun

6. Puppy love

Take your family to a local animal shelter, humane society, or pet store. Have fun looking at all the animals. Give family members the task of selecting an animal that best represents their own personality.

7. World's best book

Go to a large bookstore and tell family members to find the best book in the store. Younger kids can team up with Mom or Dad. Split up and meet back at an agreed-upon spot in 20 minutes. Family members can come up with their own criteria, selecting any book they think is best. When you gather back together, each family member presents the selected book and makes the case for why it's the best.

8. Family dinner

Tour a local farmers' market with your family, then let them know they must spontaneously purchase ingredients for tonight's dinner. Give the family a budget, and work together to decide on items. Afterward, have fun creatively cooking at home!

9. Pretend gift-giving

Hit the mall and give each person $50 in play money. Explain that each person gets to pretend to buy something from the mall as a gift for another family member. They can choose something wonderful, fun, silly, or outrageous—anything they think would make a great gift for their assigned person. Assign each person another family member to "buy" a gift for, decide on a meeting spot, set a time to gather back together, then split up and start window shopping! (If kids are young, have them pair up with parents.) When you meet up after shopping, tour the mall while family members show each other the gifts they chose and explain why.

Fun in the Great Outdoors

10. Watch the birdie

Borrow several pairs of binoculars from friends and stock up on a few bird-watching books. Then get up early one morning and take the family on a walk through a local nature preserve or bird sanctuary. Work together to identify birds, and keep a list of the birds you see. If your kids like this activity, you can keep a running list of birds you spot on each walk.

11. Spring flowers

When springtime hits, head to a garden store and allot each family member a budget of $5 to select a plant or a bed of flowers. Let everyone choose a plant. Then plant the flowers together in your yard.

12. The fork in the road

Put a spin on family walks through the neighborhood by taking along a penny. Each time you come to a corner, a family member tosses the penny. If it lands on heads, turn right; if it lands on tails, turn left. This fun tradition will lead you on a different pathway each time!

13. Teamwork

Find a lake or reservoir and go canoeing together in pairs! Many parks rent canoes and life jackets for a minimal price. Bring along sack lunches to enjoy in the canoe as you look at local wildlife.

14. Natural personalities

Visit a park and get to know each other better by playing this simple game: Select one person, such as Mom, and give the other family members five minutes to find an item in nature that reminds them of Mom. For example, family members could find a tree with beautiful flowers that reminds them of Mom's love, grab a rock that's the same color as Mom's eyes, or Pick up an acorn because Mom loves to eat nuts! Play several rounds so you can focus on and celebrate each family member.

15. Frosty's family

If you live in the Snowbelt, bundle up the family on a snowy day and head out to a local park with some snowman-making supplies. Take shovels, spray bottles filled with water, food coloring, and carrots. Your family's mission is to populate the park with snowmen, creating as many as you can in one outing. It will be quite an accomplishment, and will provide a laugh for people who drive by.

16. Daytime camping

Load up the cooler and pack up the tent for a daytime camping trip! Eat breakfast, lunch, and dinner at a campsite. Between meals, lounge around in the tent, playing board games or goofing around. When twilight hits, drive home and enjoy the comfort of your own beds.

Out-to-Eat Adventures

17. World-tour Fridays

Make weekend dinners a family adventure. Each Friday—or any day that works best for you—take your family out to eat at a different ethnic restaurant. Learn about the world and try new and exciting foods! Try to find at least one restaurant to represent each continent.

18. Food road trip

Get a copy of *Roadfood* by Jane and Michael Stern (Broadway; revised edition, 2005) or check out splendidtable.publicradio.org/whereweeat or www.roadfood.com. Find a greasy-spoon or out-of-the-way diner in your state. Plan a day trip to check it out. While you're in the car, play some fun car games like 20 Questions.

19. The best playground ever

If you have young kids, give them the mission of finding the best playground ever. Regularly take afternoon trips for sundaes or shakes to local fast-food restaurants that have play areas. After each visit, ask your children if it was the best playground or if they like the playground at a different fast-food restaurant better. Invite kids to talk about why they like each playground, which parts are the most fun, and so on.

20. Just *eat* it

See how well your family members know each other by going to a favorite restaurant and giving everyone the task of ordering a meal for the person on the right. No hints! Your whole family must do their best to order something the person will really like. And when the food arrives, no complaining is allowed!

Faith-Inspired Fun

21. Special delivery

As your family bakes several batches of cookies together, talk about the importance of encouraging people. Grab your church directory and invite each family member to choose a friend to encourage. When everyone has picked someone, plan a driving route and pack up the cookies on paper plates. As a family, drive to each house and drop off the cookies. Prompt your kids to share encouraging messages like "God loves you!" when they drop off the treats. Of course, call ahead to make sure people are home.

22. Picturing family values

Grab a few disposable cameras and spend the day at a park or in the city. Assign each family member the job of thinking about your family's values:

- What's really important in your family?
- What beliefs and principles are central to your family?

Once you've decided on a few values, each person should try to take photos of items that represent those values in some way. For example, a towering cloud might represent prayer, or two children playing together could represent love. After a few hours, head to the one-hour photo studio and get the film developed. Let each photographer look at his or her own pictures first, then have everyone share their photos and explain what they represent.

23. Food pantry shopping

Decide with your spouse on an amount of money your family will donate to a food pantry or soup kitchen. But instead of just giving money, make it a family event. Go to the grocery store together and explain to your kids the types of items the ministry needs. Then give each child a part of the budget and shop together, letting children pick out what they'd like to donate. Once you think you've spent the budgeted amount, buy the groceries and go as a family to the ministry to drop them off. Before you leave the ministry's parking lot, pray together for those who'll use the items your family picked out.

10 Time-Management Tips and Techniques

Time management is vital if you want your ministry to be effective. However, as a pastor, you can't be completely inflexible when it comes to your calendar or watch. Sometimes interruptions and impositions are God-given opportunities. Mark 1:45 tells us that so many people wanted to be with Jesus that he had to get away somewhere. Yet when he saw the multitude, he had compassion on them, stopped what he had planned, and ministered to them. He even fed them.

With that idea of ministry tucked away, the following suggestions can help you make the most of your time.

1. Use a personal calendar or electronic "assistant"

The first step is admitting that you have a problem. Acknowledge that your brain can't keep up with everything you need to accomplish. Use some method—a paper calendar or a PDA (personal digital assistant)—to keep track of your schedule, to-do items, projects, addresses, phone numbers, and e-mail addresses.

2. Keep one version of the truth

Whatever method you use, be sure that you keep just one calendar. You might be tempted to have a desk calendar at work, a day planner to carry with you, and a refrigerator calendar at home—not to mention the overall church calendar and school calendar. But if you maintain all of these, just try and schedule an appointment! You'll need to check all possible places where appointments can be kept. One version of the truth means keeping every event that affects you and your family and your ministry on one calendar. Of course, this can make for a very busy calendar. But you have to choose between a busy calendar or being busy checking each calendar.

3. Create one place for to-do lists

Where do you record all the tasks you need to tackle in a given day? You might have sticky notes, pieces of paper in your wallet, and a legal pad on your desk or dresser. Maybe you keep different to-do lists in your daily calendar pages or in your head. Maybe all of the above is true in your life, and tasks you need to work on are coming at you from every direction.

The answer is to keep one to-do list and review your list on a regular basis. Find a copy of *Getting Things Done* by David Allen (Penguin Books, 2003). Read the book and then put it into practice.

4. Create a perpetual calendar

When do you start planning for the Christmas holidays? When do you schedule the all-church work day? Make a simple perpetual calendar by creating a document listing the 12 months of the year. Under each month, create two columns titled "Events" and "Planning." Under the "Events" category, list every program or event that begins during this month. You can also include information such as the start date or duration. Under the "Planning" heading, record every program or event occurring later that you need to begin planning for during this month. For example, here's what the January page of a perpetual calendar might include.

January

Events	*Planning*
Youth winter advance (long school weekend)	Good Friday service
Men's winter Bible study (12 weeks)	Fall missions conference
Racial Harmony Sunday (second Sunday)	Vacation Bible school
Basketball tournament outreach (last weekend)	

---

5. Use project and event task lists

For major projects or big events at your church, create a list of tasks and deadlines for all that needs to be accomplished in the days and weeks preceding an event. Each year, the tasks stay essentially the same and you only need to change the responsible individuals and the deadlines. For example, the task list for a spring missions conference might look something like this:

Task	Responsibility	Deadline
Final decision on conference theme	Committee	9/15
Final decision on conference schedule	Committee	10/15
Presentation of conference logo etc.	Thomas	11/15
Congregation letter	Pastor	1/15
Bulletin insert #1	Beth	1/21
Posters in church	Sharon	1/28
Announcements begin	Rick	1/28
Sign-up sheets for men's breakfast	Will	3/1

6. Sharpen the sword

Be aware of new management books and tools. Although you can't read everything, stay in the loop regarding what people are buzzing about. Glance through the business sections of newspapers and magazines, search Amazon's top business books, and browse the preview pages the site often provides. Set the goal of reading at least one book a year that will challenge you in time management or setting priorities in life.

7. Find a mentor

As you and your church grow, your responsibilities might gradually change. Look for mentors to give you advice. Don't scare them with "Will you mentor me?" Just ask if you can take them to lunch to pick their brains. If they help you, ask if you can get together again. Ask practical questions about how they handle their workload, stay balanced, delegate responsibilities, and other issues that cross over into your life. Ask some big questions, such as "What would you do differently if you could start all over?" or "What would your priorities be if you were still my age?"

8. Go e-mail

Almost everyone has a computer and an e-mail account. Why not deal with some decisions with an e-mail meeting? Send an e-mail that clearly states what you're asking for and remind everyone to respond by "replying to all." For example, you might send an e-mail like the following to your church board or missions committee: "Can we approve giving $250 to the Wilson family to replace their tires before beginning their mission conference circuit?" If everyone responds with a "yes," consider the item approved and record the decision in the committee's official minutes. If anyone raises an objection, you can simply postpone discussion until the next meeting.

9. Hold planning sessions

A planning session looks at the big picture. Take a day away from the office to avoid interruptions. If you're short on funds, find a comfortable nook at a local coffee shop or get permission to use a classroom in another church for a day. Think through the coming year. Create an overview for a leadership-training program. Plan your preaching schedule for the next year. Tackle those longer-term tasks that never seem to get focused attention.

10. Remember to dream

"Where there is no vision, the people perish" (Proverbs 29:18, King James Version). Take some time to dream about the future. What are your dreams for yourself, your church, your staff, the church leaders, your family?

27 Quick Pick-Me-Ups

Do you feel as if you're always on call? Do people in your church come to you first when they need encouragement, a listening ear, or a shoulder to cry on? If so, you're blessed! Your compassion for others is part of why you became a pastor. However, you've also got sermons to write, marriages to officiate, staff to facilitate, buildings to repair, funds to acquire! Even the most "with-it" pastors occasionally feel like they're going to crash and burn. So when stresses hit, consider the following pick-me-ups to revitalize your mind and body.

1. Schedule bits of personal escape time

Schedule short bursts of time for yourself on the calendar at the beginning of each week. Honor this appointment as you would any other. Whether you just shut the office door and turn off the lights for quiet seclusion or leave the building for a 15-minute walk, these quick escapes will provide moments of peace and allow you to clear your head.

2. Read for enjoyment

How about a good mystery or thriller? Make a date with your local bookstore and peruse the shelves. Or get online and browse. Once you make a purchase, indulge yourself by reading a chapter or two a day.

3. Get up and move

Take the stairs, park your car farther from the building, ride your bike, play a sport you enjoy. Stress and anxiety will subside as you use your muscles. And in the long run, you'll be in better shape, feel better, and look better!

4. Join a health club

Want something more regimented? Often, paying for the use of a gym will give you the incentive you need to make your workouts more consistent.

5. Plan a family hike

Pack a picnic lunch, gather the family, and head for the hills (or at least the park). Walk, rest, and enjoy a meal without interruption out in God's miraculous gift of nature. Be sure to turn off your cell phone.

6. Eat well

Substituting cookies and brownies for sandwiches or skipping meals may seem easy. But to nourish others in faith you must first nourish yourself physically. Pack a nutritious lunch before you leave the house, complete with a healthy snack for later in the day.

7. Make a date with your spouse

If you're married, meet your spouse for lunch, or just to sit at a coffee shop and catch up with each other.

8. Play

If you have kids, take them to a favorite playground or amusement park. As you experience the rides or attractions, leave behind your worries.

9. Stretch

Push back from your desk, stand up, and reach your arms for the ceiling. Touch your toes, twist at the waist, and feel your muscles relax.

10. Write

Whether on the computer or the old-fashioned way, keep a journal of the high points in your ministry—times when you knew it was all worth the hard work. Look for the silver lining behind the moments when you weren't sure. Reread your journal entries when you need an even quicker pick-me-up.

11. Give yourself a treat

Whether your preference is Starbucks or Krispy Kreme, indulge your taste buds once in a while without guilt. (Just make sure your treat doesn't become a habit!)

12. Plan a midweek getaway

Leave town completely, or just pull the curtains shut at home and hibernate with a good book. Plan to be unavailable for a couple of days to wind down. Ask a staff member or lay leader to cover your responsibilities.

13. Rediscover an old hobby

Dust off old baseball cards, train sets, and bird-watching books. Scout around for bridge players, softball teams, and weekday runners.

14. Discover a new hobby

Try something you've always wanted to tackle but couldn't find the time. Surf the Web and magazines for information, ideas, and resources. Check the newspaper for local groups and attend a meeting. Sample first, and decide later if you want to participate.

15. Play an instrument you learned as a child

Maybe you'll actually *want* to practice this time, now that your mom isn't watching over your shoulder. Or you could learn a new instrument, without anyone forcing you to play.

16. Call a friend you haven't seen in years

Catch up on the recent stuff and relive the good old days. Exchange e-mail addresses and keep in touch every few weeks or so.

17. Grow a plant

Put the container in your office window and watch the miracle of life materialize before your eyes. As you care for your seedling, concentrate on all the little miracles God places in your life.

18. Clean out your closet

Even work like this offers a change of pace that can freshen a dreary day. Donate your castoffs to the Salvation Army or Goodwill. Or choose something you love from your closet and donate it to a local clothing bank.

19. Keep a photo album

Organize your photos of vacation spots and other places you've been. Or purchase some travel magazines, tear out photos, and create an album of places you'd like to see.

20. Write a list of your blessings

After you've written down the ways God has been blessing you and your family, put the list in an envelope and send it to yourself. When it arrives, open it and enjoy the blessings again.

21. Bend a sympathetic listening ear

Seek out a good friend, your spouse, another pastor, or anyone you feel comfortable opening up with. Talk about yourself for a change. Voice your concerns, your dreams, and your aspirations.

22. Do a crossword puzzle

Really work at it until you finish or get stumped. Then ask others to help or look at the solution key.

23. Write a short story

Create a character and a story about someone like you. See how your character works through difficult times. Provide a happy ending.

24. Send e-cards to special friends or family members

There are many e-card Web sites available, and many of them are free of charge. Break up your day and others' as well by sending them an e-card. Check your e-mail throughout the day as you anticipate a response.

25. Spend time in the public library

Choose a new author or new series, rent a movie or CD, or ask about the classes or workshops they offer. Borrow a foreign language tape and learn while you're driving. Or just relax and read the newspaper or a magazine you don't subscribe to.

26. Give yourself a little credit

God chose you to be a leader in his church here on earth because he knows you can handle it. Thank God for putting his faith in you— and especially for uniquely equipping you for the ministry you're involved in.

27. Delegate

Encourage others to take leadership roles within the church community. Learn to recognize your own signs of burnout, and assign tasks to others before you feel the fires of fatigue licking at your heels. Set high expectations, and be ready for people to surpass them.

CROSS REFERENCE:
Also see "12 Ways to Identify and Encourage Leaders," Section 7, page 195.

Section 6:
Congregational Care

Your church is made up of a lot of different programs and activities—worship, sermons, children's programs, youth groups, community service. But most of all: *Your church is your people.* And the main purpose of pastoral ministry is to glorify God by caring for those people. Some days, that will come easily. Other days won't be so easy. But the rewards of investing in your people—your church—far outweigh the difficulties. The ideas in this section will help breathe life into your ministry and, as you use them, into the lives of those whom God has entrusted to your care.

Section 6: Table of Contents

30 Great Questions to Start Conversations and Keep Them Going

It's easy to start a conversation. Just ask, "Hey, how's it going?" or "How are you doing?" Suddenly you're involved in an actual conversation. You're not too deep into the conversation, but it's begun. Of course, as a pastor, you usually need to move beyond this point.

If you want to improve your skills at keeping conversations going, here's a strategy. Think of a matrix. On the horizontal axis you'll find *question starters,* the old reliable "five W's and H" you learned in English or journalism class long ago: Who, What, When, Where, Why, and How. On the vertical axis, you'll find *content indicators,* various aspects of a person's life: Personal, Family, Work or School, Church, and Groups or Associations. You'll find a host of questions wherever two points intersect. Here's a sample question at each of these 30 intersections to whet your appetite:

Personal Questions

1. Who & Personal:

Can you tell me a little about yourself, what makes you tick?

2. What & Personal:

What's your passion; what do you really love to do?

3. When & Personal:

When did you first move to this area?

4. Where & Personal:

Where are you on your spiritual journey?

5. Why & Personal:

What inspires you and why do you think that is?

6. How & Personal:

How are you wired?

Family Questions

7. Who & Family:

Who are you in your family—firstborn, middle child, "the baby"?

8. What & Family:

What traditions did you have growing up, and are they still as much a part of your family today?

9. When & Family:

When did you venture out on your own for the first time?

10. Where & Family:

Where does your family go to get away from it all?

11. Why & Family:

Why are you glad you live in this city (or state)?

12. How & Family:

How does your family stay balanced in this busy world?

Work or School Questions

13. Who & Work or School:

Who do people at your work (or school) say you are?

14. What & Work or School:

What keeps you busy between weekends?

15. When & Work or School:

When did you begin your job (or studies)?

16. Where & Work or School:

Where do you work (or study)?

17. Why & Work or School:

Why do you enjoy your job (or studies) so much?

18. How & Work or School:

How did you decide upon that profession (or school)?

Church Questions

19. Who & Church:
Who have you connected with here at church?

20. What & Church:
What part of the worship service really hits home with you?

21. When & Church:
When did you start attending here?

22. Where & Church:
Where did your spiritual journey begin?

23. Why & Church:
Why do you believe this church is a good fit for you?

24. How & Church:
How can this church better meet your spiritual needs?

Group or Association Questions

25. Who & Groups or Associations:
Who do you really enjoy hanging out with?

26. What & Groups or Associations:
What groups are you a part of, and what roles do you play?

27. When & Groups or Associations:
When do you really enjoy getting together with others?

28. Where & Groups or Associations:
Where do these gatherings take place?

29. Why & Groups or Associations:
Why do you feel it's important for you to be involved in the particular groups or associations you're in?

30. How & Groups or Associations:
How did you first become involved?

19 Courageous Ways to Encourage Church Members

Encouragement is more valuable than you can imagine. When you encourage others, you follow in the spirit of Barnabas. Although his real name was Joseph, he was called Barnabas because it meant "Son of Encouragement" (Acts 4:36). Being an encourager doesn't come naturally for some people. However, if you encourage others, you're likely to increase the "encouragement quotient" in your congregation—and the amount you receive in your own life.

In that spirit, try the following courageous ways to encourage church members—courageous, because *encouragement* literally means, "to fill with courage."

1. Preach the Word

Your greatest encouragement to the people of your church will come directly from God's Word.

2. Know and greet people by name

Sure, it's difficult to remember each person's name, and some churches use name tags to help. Go out among the congregation at some time before, during, or after the service to greet church members (by name, whenever possible). While you can't greet everyone, you can greet some. As others look on, they'll be encouraged that the pastor is "out among us." It communicates that you're available and approachable in times of need.

3. Pray

Tell people that you're praying for them. Make it natural, of course. Listen for prayer concerns or pray generally. When you bump into people, let them know how you're praying for them.

4. Encourage

You can also let people know you're thinking about them by making a phone call or sending an e-mail, note, or card. These expressions of encouragement can come on birthdays and anniversaries, or at times of joy or struggles in their lives, such as at the birth of a child or when a church member has just come through surgery.

5. Take a personal interest

Make note of the success of those people who live God-honoring lives. One easy way to do this is to put resources in their hands. It might be a gift or a loan, but let church members know you care about what's going on in their lives with just the right resource: a pamphlet on how to have a great quiet time, a CD of an inspirational message, a spiritual-growth book that's "just right" for where they are in their spiritual journey.

6. Connect

You can't have breakfast, lunch, dinner, and morning and afternoon coffee with church members every day. But you can set aside a day or two a week to schedule such meetings. Give the people of your church opportunities to share a vision, ask for advice, or be there to encourage you.

7. Listen

As you practice the discipline of listening, you'll be a great encouragement to church members. They're more concerned about how much you care than how much you know.

8. Counsel

Even if you're not the primary counselor in your church, or if you're unable to hold regular hours for counseling, people will come to you for advice. The greatest advice you have to offer will be based directly on God's Word. Take classes on biblical counseling to become more comfortable with this, if you need to.

9. Empower

Let the people of your congregation know what it takes to start a ministry at the church. Remember, a central aspect of your pastoral role is "to prepare God's people for works of service, so that the body of Christ may be built up" (Ephesians 4:12).

10. Have fun

Do what families do together—they play and have fun with each other! Go on picnics, have barbecues, do the potluck thing. Share memories, tell stories, tease and joke with one another. Be sure that "fun" is part of the church calendar.

11. Connect your people to one another

God's people need to connect with God's people. For example, someone might approach you with a vision for a new ministry, and perhaps you know of someone else with a similar dream. Or someone expresses a passion for outdoor adventure, and you know of someone else with the same passion. Encourage them by connecting them with one another.

12. Be real

Whether it's in a message or when you get together with church members, share who you really are. Relate personal experiences that help church members get closer to you—who you are and the person God hard-wired you to be.

13. Give recognition

Sometimes this happens publicly, recognizing key volunteers for their works of service within the church, or acknowledging church members for their accomplishments in the congregation or in the community. At other times, your recognition might be private and personal, whether face to face or in a call, card, or e-mail. In particular, look for people who are serving in almost invisible ways. Let them know that you appreciate their efforts to serve in unique, behind-the-scenes, yet crucial ministries. Show appreciation with a handwritten letter, a gift, or certificate of appreciation—whatever's appropriate.

CROSS REFERENCE:
Also see "32 Ways to Encourage Staff and Volunteers," Section 7, page 172.

14. Give credit where credit's due

If someone passes along a key illustration, verse, or passage that you use in a sermon, ask permission from the source to use his or her name. This will encourage congregation members to see that you care enough about them to listen to what's on their hearts.

15. Challenge church members to become engaged

You've heard of the 80/20 rule—that 80 percent of the people in church allow the other 20 percent to do the ministry. Help your members realize that God has given them gifts, talents, abilities, and experiences to serve others. Ask, "What are you doing to make a difference that will last beyond your life and into eternity?" If an answer comes quickly, give them an affirming pat on the back. If they don't have an answer, challenge them: "Where in the world has God given you a passion to serve? What has he put on your heart?"

CROSS REFERENCE:
Also see "12 Ways to Identify and Encourage Leaders," Section 7, page 195.

16. Volunteer alongside people

Let the people of your church see your heart for the church's ministry beyond what they see you accomplish in the pulpit. Help park cars. Serve as an usher. Wash cars with the youth group. Mix cement and pound nails on the Habitat for Humanity project. Visit prisoners with the outreach team. Take a turn in the latte bar. Simply serving alongside church members will help them see the true you, and they'll certainly be encouraged in the process!

17. Connect with a small group

You need your own small group. You need your own advisers. You need individuals you can journey through life with, seek advice from, and bounce ideas off. Be teachable. Allow these select church members who really know you to correct you. Thank them when they do.

18. Encourage church members to encourage one another

It's biblical, and it's critical. Consider all of the "one another/each other" verses in Scripture, and help your congregation to consider them, too. Put them in the church bulletin. Preach them. Use them to open your devotionals with your leaders. Put them on banners and decorate your sanctuary with them.

19. Never give up!

You'll always see needs among you. Remember that the people of your church are watching. If you get exasperated or give up, they will, too. They'll become discouraged and lack the strength it takes to press on. Instead, see the needs around you, and take the lead in engaging, equipping, and empowering church members to address these needs in God-honoring ways.

6 Counseling Helps When People Are Hurting or Grieving

Counseling is a critical ministry in the church. The following suggestions will help you successfully care for people who are hurting and grieving.

1. Pray for guidance

Seek God's guidance and ask him how much counseling he wants you to take on. Counseling is demanding, and God doesn't call every pastor to provide in-depth counseling. Ask God to give you wisdom to provide excellent counseling services for your congregation and at the same time set healthy boundaries, delegate care, and protect you from burning out. Two specific areas where you need God's guidance:

- Ask God to guide you before you commit to any counseling relationship. When people grieve, you'll naturally feel compelled to help. But only God knows the best plan to relieve their suffering, and that plan might not involve you. God might lead you to simply listen, encourage, and pray with them, and then link them with mature Christians, mentors, or professionals who can offer longer-term help.
- Pray for guidance when you meet with people in need. Encourage the people you're counseling to place their trust in God and not lean too much on you.

2. Develop support networks in your congregation

People who are hurting or grieving need a lot of support. Beneficial resources include: counselors, caring friends, mentors, support groups, small groups, and Bible studies. Combine church, medical, and community services as needed to help an individual back into life. Work to make the following kinds of support available:

- Train mature Christians to care for hurting and grieving people. Develop mentoring, discipling, and advising relationships and programs within your church.
- Form support groups for people who are hurting and grieving. Recruit a leader who has walked through grief victoriously. Encourage the leader to pray for guidance at the start of each meeting; include a short teaching to give participants hope in God's resources; ask different group members to teach when they're ready—people recover more quickly when they start to help others. The foundations of Christian support groups should include relying on God, respecting confidentiality, and fostering mutual support.

3. Listen with your heart

People want you to listen, but that can be tough when they just want attention. Listening is one of most powerful ways you can show love. You listen not just with your ears but with your heart. Although it's tough to listen if you don't care about a topic, it's easy to listen when you care about the person speaking. Some ways to listen with your heart:

- Listen past the words. Listen to the emotions erupting from the heart. The burdens, anxiety, hurt, or confusion he or she carries is what you need to address. Don't get so engrossed in problem solving that you forget to listen to the cries of the heart. Even if you're dealing with a complainer, realize that the problem might stem from a desperate heart. If the person senses that you and God care, the complaints might vanish.
- People believe they have your undivided attention if you turn to face them, make eye contact, respond at appropriate times, and don't cross your arms or legs. You can show you are "with" them by subtly mirroring the positions of their bodies. Keep your heart open to God's love for each person and your spiritual ears open to hear God's guidance for your conversation.
- Listening with love is the foundation of counseling. Be sure to listen to people first, and always speak the truth in love. Pray for God's guidance and be gentle with people in emotional pain, just as you would be careful with someone with physical wounds.

4. Be comfortable with tears

Keep tissues handy. If counselees start crying, simply hand them tissues and listen. Crying can be a healthy release and signal a breakthrough. So, let people cry for a while. Some things to keep in mind:

- Look for chronic and protracted crying binges. A day of crying can be a day of deliverance if the person releases long-held burdens and opens his or her heart to God's help. But if crying continues unabated, it's a sign the person needs to be referred for professional help.
- Watch for signs of severe depression. While reeling from the shock of a husband's or wife's leaving or the death of a loved one, a bereaved person may become severely depressed or even suicidal. If someone you're counseling expresses suicidal wishes, get that person to a doctor, psychiatrist, or hospital emergency room for professional evaluation and safety.
- Don't minimize suffering. Emotions are a normal and healthy part of human existence. People experience intense emotions

after loss. They often need counseling when they experience several losses in a short time. Emotions can build until the normal supports of friends and family aren't enough. Reassure anyone seeking counseling that they're wise to seek help.

• Support counselees with your faith that God is good. He answers prayer. Remind them nothing is impossible with God. Infuse hope. Listen and show you care before you offer scriptural guidelines. Pray that God will give people wisdom to make decisions. Direct them to the only One who totally understands, knows the best course for their futures, and heals hearts.

5. Observe professional guidelines

Form relationships with Christian counselors, doctors, and psychiatrists in your area so you know exactly where to refer people when necessary. Find professionals with high standards, good references, and a Christian approach to counseling. Whenever you feel overwhelmed with counseling, the wisest thing to do is call for experienced help. Here are some thoughts about specific counseling situations and when to refer issues to counseling professionals:

• When people share their hearts in counseling, they expect what they say to be kept confidential. Don't share stories without consent.

• If you counsel the opposite sex or children, make sure another adult is in the room or that your door has a window with a secretary in view. Guard against emotional transference—when a counselee becomes overly attached to a counselor. Don't be unkind, but keep boundaries in place. Refer the person to another counselor, if necessary.

• Don't discourage people from seeking professional care. Counselors, doctors, and psychiatrists provide crucial services, and hospitalization is sometimes the only way to keep a suicidal person safe.

• Consider using a term such as "mentors" or "disciplers" for your church's lay counselors. This avoids the connotation that they're providing professional counseling (and minimizes potential liabilities).

• If counselees are homicidal—threatening to harm or kill another person—you're responsible to notify appropriate authorities and warn people who might be in danger.

• If you aren't sure about the counseling issues that you or your church might be liable for, consider taking a counseling and ethics course at an area college. View the current American Counseling Association's Code of Ethics at www.cacd .org/codeofethics.html. The American Association of Pastoral Counselors Code of Ethics is posted at www.aapc.org/ethics.htm.

6. Give your own burdens to God

You can't help others if you're going under. Counseling is a high-maintenance activity. Avoid burnout by praying for guidance, respecting your limits of time and energy, and delegating. Be sensitive to the condition of your heart. If you feel overwhelmed, here are some suggestions:

- Cut down on watching news. Know your limits. Pay attention to how much counseling and bad news you can handle before you start to sink emotionally.

- Choose positive friends. If counseling is weighing down your heart, then you need to spend time with friends who lift you up.

CROSS REFERENCE:
Also see "27 Quick Pick-Me-Ups," Section 5, page 138, and "23 Fun and Simple Family Getaways and Events," Section 5, page 129.

- Give yourself permission to enjoy life. Go fishing, spend family time at the beach, laugh, tell jokes, and have fun. Free time can be extremely profitable, if you relax, let go of burdens, and allow God to refresh and inspire you.

- Spend more time alone with the Lord. No one can lift you up like he can. Run to him. He's always waiting to pour out his love on you. Even counselors are called only to carry light burdens. Heavy burdens belong to the Lord.

CROSS REFERENCE:
Also see "2 Self-Directed Retreats," Section 5, page 112.

- Don't try to fix people. If you remind yourself that only God can heal, you'll spare yourself many burdens. You're responsible to teach, guide, and encourage, but only God can change hearts. Remind the people you counsel that you're not the answer. Connect them with caring Christians and guide them to the Father.

9 Tips for Hospital Visits

Perhaps nothing you do in your ministry is more important than personal contact with the people of your church. While this can throw you into uncomfortable situations, it's also where you can make the most difference in people's lives. The following ideas will help you make the most of visiting people in the hospital and other care-giving facilities.

1. Check your attitude, feelings, and emotions

Conduct a quick spiritual-attitude check before you enter a patient's room. Pause in your car before entering the hospital or stop in the hospital chapel for a brief time of prayer before making the visit.

2. Make the visit comfortable

Enter the room with a warm smile and a friendly greeting. Say a few words of encouragement but be careful not to give medical advice. Even simple phrases such as "It will all work out" or "You'll be feeling better in no time" might not be true. While you want to show genuine concern for the individual, focus on conversation that you'd have if the individual wasn't in the hospital. Be natural.

CROSS REFERENCE:

Also see "30 Great Questions to Start Conversations and Keep Them Going" in this section, page 144.

3. Don't stay too long

But don't make it seem that you're rushing away, either. Aim to stay for about 15 to 20 minutes.

4. Be sensitive

Try to read a patient's attitude, feelings and emotions, and physical comfort. Even if you spent an hour driving to visit one patient, make sure he or she is up for the visit. Offer to return if he or she doesn't feel up to having visitors.

5. Meet spiritual needs

Of course, your role is as a spiritual provider. You offer spiritual strength and encouragement to people in need. Be sure to be sensitive to the spiritual needs of those you're visiting.

6. Accept the person as he or she is

Use "reflective listening." Reflect back what you hear the person saying or sense in his or her feelings. For example, "It sounds like you're feeling discouraged today," and then follow up with a word of encouragement. Accept the patient's feelings and attitudes.

7. Respect the patient

Always be positive even when it is difficult. You may not appreciate what you hear, but respect their feelings.

8. Encourage the patient

Reading Scripture, speaking a few words of encouragement, and praying for the patient are the best encouragement you can provide. However, always ask the patient's permission to read Scripture or pray, and honor the individual's response.

9. Before surgery

When someone is hospitalized for surgery, nurses typically have a lot of questions for the patient. When you arrive, check in with the nurse's station, identify yourself as the patient's pastor, and ask if you may visit the patient. If a nurse needs to ask the patient questions, simply excuse yourself and return after the nurse leaves. Respect the patient's privacy.

10 THINGS *NOT* TO DO WHEN MAKING HOSPITAL VISITS:

These rules also apply to visitations at hospices, assisted-living centers, nursing homes, or care centers.

1. Don't disobey posted signs. For example, if a sign says "no visitors," check with the nurse's station.

2. Don't forget your role. You're not a nurse, doctor, psychologist, social worker, financial planner, time manager, lawyer, or family member. Remember that you're the pastor and need to stay in that role.

3. Don't serve the Lord's Supper without permission from the patient's nurse. In some situations you could cause serious problems by giving even a small amount of food or drink.

4. Don't be negative. Sometimes that's difficult, but with God's help you can be positive in all situations.

5. Don't be the focus of conversation. Talk about the patient and his or her needs. Don't compare your past experiences with whatever surgery or illness the patient is experiencing.

6. Don't try to outtalk the person. Instead, ask questions to draw out the patient.

7. Don't talk constantly. Some silence is fine. If the patient seems tired, offer to pray. When you leave, you can add, "I'll stop back and see you [day]."

8. Don't compare the patient's situation with others or offer solutions. Remember, you're not a nurse, doctor, psychologist, or social worker.

9. Don't try to organize the person. Remember, you're not a financial planner, time manager, lawyer, or family member.

10. Don't be unnatural. You don't have to pretend to be any more "superspiritual" than you naturally are. Just be yourself.

9 Reminders for Dealing With Deaths and Funerals

As a pastor, you'll inevitably face dying and death. You will be called upon to conduct funerals. Although it's been said that our culture "doesn't do death well," you can use the following ways to help families through the difficult days surrounding a loved one's death and funeral service.

1. Prepare your own heart

When you hear of someone's death or receive a request to conduct a funeral, spend time in prayer and quiet reflection before you meet with the family.

2. Contact the family

Personally visit the family, pray, and leave helpful literature. One book you can keep copies of to leave with a hurting family is *Healing Takes Time* by David Gallagher (Liturgical Press, 2005).

3. Don't meddle in family personal affairs

Usually, it's not a good idea for the pastor to accompany the family to select a casket or get involved in family financial decisions. If you're asked to recommend a funeral home, provide a few suggestions. However, don't make negative comments about funeral homes, hospitals, hospice centers, or any other health-care facilities. At the request of the family, you can meet with them at the funeral home. But excuse yourself when the discussion moves toward financial issues.

4. Gain as much information as possible

When you meet with the family, encourage them to share both practical information and warm memories that might help you prepare for the funeral or memorial service and graveside service. Certainly, you won't share anything negative about the deceased at the services. (Also see the "Funeral Information Guide" in the Congregational-Care Forms at the end of this section, page 163.)

5. Use Scripture

Read a passage of Scripture when you meet with the family. Use comforting and encouraging Scriptures—such as Psalm 139:6-12; Matthew 5:3-8; or 1 Corinthians 15:20-26—during the funeral or memorial service.

6. Determine if the family wants to be involved in the service

Be careful that emotions don't get out of hand. Offer to read a brief note or letter to make the service more personal. Discourage open sharing during a memorial service. Instead, suggest that family and close friends have a time of sharing before the service (during a visitation or viewing time) or afterward at a meal.

7. Provide a simple order of service

Include prayer, Scripture reading, a brief eulogy, music, a brief message, a committal, and a benediction. Most funeral services should last 30 minutes to one hour. The graveside service should only last about 10 minutes; include prayer, Scripture reading, some committal words, and a benediction.

8. Follow up with the family

A few days after the service, call to ask family members if you can stop by. Take along a gift of food—perhaps a basket of fruit or a tray of breakfast pastries. This is a good opportunity to invite unchurched people to visit your church. Place notes in your calendar to send cards or notes to the family each month for several months.

9. Offer grief support

If your church offers a grief support group, invite the family members to participate. If your church doesn't offer this type of group, suggest community agencies or other churches that offer something similar.

3 Guidelines for Wedding Ceremonies

Pastors have the unique blessing of officiating at weddings. You get to be a part of a couple's most joyous and memorable occasion. While a wedding is a celebration, your pastoral role should also include making a couple aware of certain logistical requirements of their wedding. The following ideas can serve as reminders of what to discuss and communicate. (Also see "Traditional Wedding Order" in the Congregational-Care Forms at the end of this section, page 165.)

1. Legal requirements

Remember that a wedding ceremony involves meeting state legal requirements. When you meet with a couple, carefully go over not only premarital counseling and the ceremony, but the requirements and process for obtaining the marriage license. Because laws can change, contact your county Clerk and Recorder office.

2. Offer premarital counseling

Meet with the engaged couple several times for counseling. Cover issues such as communication, conflict resolution, and financial planning in premarital counseling sessions. If you're qualified, offer testing such as the Taylor-Johnson Temperament Analysis. Or refer the couple to a licensed Christian marriage and family counselor or a Christian psychologist.

3. Plan and organize

Carefully go over exactly what the couple wants in their ceremony—music, candles, guests, how the bride will enter. Write down everything so you don't forget or confuse one couple's wishes with another. (Also see "Wedding Information" in the Congregational-Care Forms at the end of this section, page 166.)

6 Do's and Don'ts for Baby Dedications

What a joy! A baby is born into a church family, and the parents ask for their child to be dedicated. Many churches have baby dedications as a brief part of a regular service—every month or every quarter. Use the following suggestions to make these dedications meaningful to the parents of the baby and your congregation.

1. DO meet with the family

Carefully go over each part of the dedication service and answer any questions.

2. DO be warm and personal

Make sure you use family members' names and the full name of the baby during the dedication service. Write everything down rather than having a public memory lapse!

3. DO offer prayer and read Scripture

As part of the dedication service, present a charge to the family and to the congregation. Choose a portion of Scripture to read—such as 1 Samuel 1:26-28 or Mark 10:13-16—and pray for the family and spiritual growth of the baby. (Also see "Baby Dedication Charges" in the Congregational-Care Forms at the end of this section, page 168.)

4. DON'T hold the baby if the child will experience trauma

Some babies will cry when held by a stranger, and a screaming infant in your arms will cause discomfort for parents and distraction for others. However, if you and the child have a comfort level, holding the child is a warm and wonderful personal touch.

5. DON'T make the dedication time too long

Again, present a brief challenge, read appropriate Scripture, and pray. With infants, timing is everything (and that timing should be short).

6. DON'T use dedication times to preach

A baby dedication is a time for celebration. Don't cause guilt or bring up negative issues. Focus on joy!

10 Ways to Assimilate New People Into Your Fellowship

When people come through the front door of your church for the first time, how do you keep them from eventually slipping out the back? Obviously, you can't hold anyone captive, so let visitors move on if your church doesn't seem like the right "fit" for them. But when visitors feel comfortable and turn into "regular attenders," use the following ideas to help these new people become active members of your church body.

1. Make a good first impression

Before you can assimilate anyone, you have to get visitors to return to your church. You might not have an opportunity to make a good second impression. The old adage is true, "perception is reality." Make sure that as visitors come into your parking lot, their very first impression is positive, and that it carries through every moment visitors are present.

RECOMMENDED RESOURCE:

First Impressions: Creating Wow Experiences in Your Church by Mark Waltz (Group)— loads of ideas to make your visitors feel embraced and accepted.

2. Make visitors a high priority

Keeping new people coming back is much more important than how many visitors your church has. You might have 50 visitors each Sunday, but what if only one or two return? It's far better to have five visitors and get all five to return. Evaluate the resources your church uses to generate visitors through advertising and holding large events against the resources you use to retain visitors.

3. Make new people feel needed, wanted, and appreciated

Words are important, and actions speak even louder. Take every possible opportunity to connect with visitors and new members. (Also see the "Encouragement Postcard" in the Congregational-Care Forms at the end of this section, page 169.)

4. Be biblical

Scripture emphasizes the importance of each part of the church body: "The whole body, being fitted and held together by what every joint supplies, according to the proper working of each individual part, causes the growth of the body for the building up of itself in love" (Ephesians 4:16, *New American Standard Bible*).

5. Set high expectations

Expect people who become part of your church to discover their spiritual gifts and use them. Everyone should know what it means to be part of the body and fully assimilated into the church.

6. Encourage small-group involvement

Promote the biblical pattern and mandate of small group involvement, "Every day they continued to meet together....They broke bread in their homes and ate together with glad and sincere hearts" (Acts 2:46).

7. Show your love and care

Loving and caring for your church means spending time with people. When you make a first-time visit, give a small, simple gift that has special meaning. For example, purchase some small toy lambs (stuffed animals) and attach a tag with a meaningful verse like Isaiah 40:11: "He tends his flock like a shepherd: He gathers the lambs in his arms and carries them close to his heart." Add your name and telephone numbers to the tag. Tell the recipients that the little lamb is a reminder that you're there any time they need you.

8. Praise your congregation

Encourage and praise your church at every turn. Celebrate strengths and achievements often. New people naturally want to join a "winning team."

9. Help people find meaningful places of service

Meaningful means that people experience the fulfillment of making a difference for eternity—that they're making real spiritual progress at their church. Help people discover their God-given gifts and learn where they can best fit in to meaningful ministries of the church.

10. Create new ministries to involve more people

As you identify more spiritual gifts and passions within your church, create new ministries and ministry positions, which will provide an increasingly rich environment for service.

Funeral Information Guide

Name of Deceased: _____

Funeral home: _____Visitation hours: _____

Day of funeral service: _____ Time: _____ Location: _____

Graveside service at: _____ Time: _____

Born
Day: _____ Date: _____ Year:_____

at (Location): _____,

Passed away
Day: _____ Date: _____ Year: _____

at _____,

Having lived _____ years.

Survived by:
(Spouse, brothers, sisters, grandchildren, great-grandchildren, etc.)

Spouse: _____

Brothers: _____ Sisters: _____

Children: _____

Grandchildren: _____

Great-grandchildren: _____

Other relatives: _____

_____

Grew up in: _____ Attended school at: _____

Military service: _____

Funeral Information Guide continued

Married for_____years

Lived in: _____

Church involvement: _____

Service clubs: _____

Hobbies: _____

Remembered most by others for: _____

Favorite music: _____

Favorite TV programs: _____

Favorite movies: _____

Favorite flowers: _____

Favorite pastimes: _____

Favorite foods: _____

Favorite verses or poems: _____

Organist: _____ Solos: _____

Meal? _____ Approximate number: _____ Location: _____

Funeral home contact: _____ Phone: _____

Any other helpful information: _____

_____

Comments: _____

_____

_____

Traditional Wedding Order

Prelude
(Option: Special music during seating of grandparents and parents)
Grandparents seated
Parents seated: groom's parents, then bride's parents

Music change when wedding party enters
Pastor enters
Groom and groomsmen enter: groom, best man, groomsmen
Bridal party enters: bridesmaids, maid of honor, flower girl, and ring bearer

Music change when bride enters
Bride enters escorted by father or both parents
Opening comments and prayer by pastor
"Who gives this woman?" question and father-of-the-bride's response
Groom steps forward to take bride; bride and groom take positions on platform
    (bride hands bouquet to maid of honor)
(Option: Special music)

Message by pastor
"I do" vows
"Repeat after me" vows
"Ring" vows
Pronouncement of husband and wife
(Option: Special music)

Pastor explains the unity candle and couple lights it
(Option: Special music)

Prayer
Groom kisses the bride (bride gets bouquet from maid of honor)
Introduction of "Mr. and Mrs." to congregation

Recessional music
Bride and groom exit, followed by wedding party
Parents exit, following the wedding party
Ushers return to usher out guests

Wedding Information

Date and time of wedding: _____

Location: _____

Date and time of rehearsal: _____

Bride's name: _____

    Bride's parents: _____

    Bride's address: _____

    Home phone: _____ Work: _____ Mobile: _____

    Date and place of birth: _____

    Religious background or affiliation: _____

    Maid/matron of honor: _____

    Bridesmaids: _____

Groom's name: _____

    Groom's parents: _____

    Groom's address: _____

    Home phone: _____ Work: _____ Mobile:_____

    Date and place of birth: _____

    Religious background or affiliation: _____

    Best Man: _____

    Groomsmen: _____

Wedding Planner: _____

    Wedding Planner's address: _____

    Work phone: _____ Mobile: _____

Wedding Information continued

Photographer: _____

    Photographer's address: _____

    Work phone: _____ Mobile: _____

    Wedding photos taken: _____

    Before ceremony: _____ During ceremony: _____ After ceremony: _____

Florist: _____

    Florist's address: _____

    Work phone: _____ Mobile: _____

Musicians: _____

_____

Location of reception: _____

    Reception open to all wedding guests: _____ By invitation only: _____

Dates placed on church calendar: Rehearsal: _____ Wedding:_____

Approximate number of guests: _____

Special Requests: _____

_____

_____

Time for the wedding party to arrive: _____

Dates of premarital counseling: _____

Baby Dedication Charges

Charge to the Parents:

"Do you [parent's names], promise in the presence of God, your friends and family, and this church body to do your best to instill in your child the values and teachings that will lead him/her to a personal relationship with Jesus Christ? Do you promise to pray regularly for your child? Do you also promise to entrust your child to God's care and to offer him/her to God for his service and ministry? If so, say, 'We do.'"

Charge to the Congregation:

"Do you, friends and members of [name of church], promise to commit your time, resources, and prayer to help these parents raise their child in a way that he/she will come to a personal relationship with Jesus Christ and grow to desire to serve God? If so, answer, 'We do.'"

Encouragement Postcard

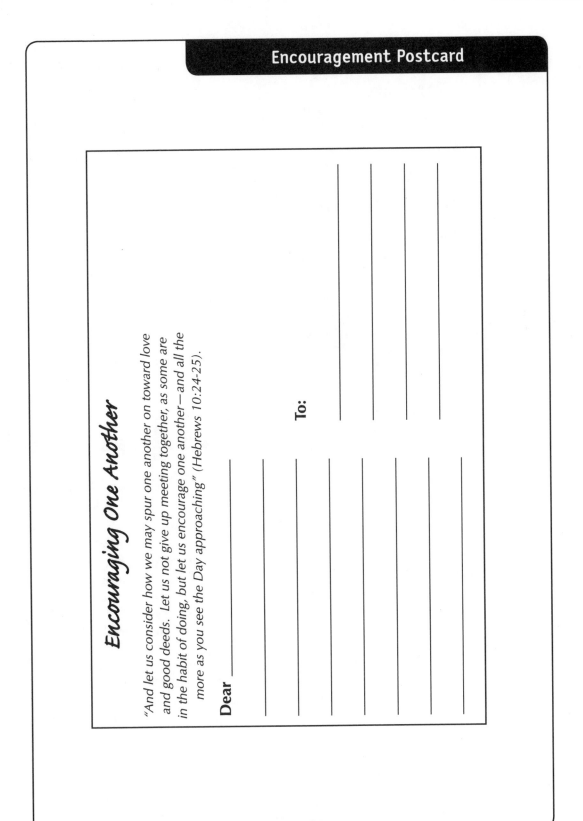

Encouraging One Another

"And let us consider how we may spur one another on toward love and good deeds. Let us not give up meeting together, as some are in the habit of doing, but let us encourage one another—and all the more as you see the Day approaching" (Hebrews 10:24-25).

Dear _____

To: _____

Section 7:
Developing
Your Leaders and
Volunteers

Some days, you might feel as if you're running your church entirely on your own. But the truth is that no pastor can "fly solo." Whether you're the only paid person on your staff or you lead a megachurch with multiple pastoral and support staff members, you need others to carry out the ministry of the church. This might be a mixture of volunteers, lay leaders (who are also volunteers, of course), support staff, and pastoral staff.

Whatever mix you have, you'll strengthen yourself and your church as you work to give away ministry. This happens when you consciously build strong volunteers, leaders, and staff members who feel that their pieces of ministry are valuable, needed, and appreciated. The ideas in this section will help you instill those feelings in all the people called to serve in your congregation.

Section 7: Table of Contents

32 Ways to Encourage Staff and Volunteers

CROSS REFERENCE:
Also see "5 Ways to Focus on Acts of Service," Section 4, page 94.

We all want to feel appreciated. The people who volunteer to serve your church are the real ministers. When you heap public attention and praise on your volunteers, it communicates that each person has a special role in the church. Use the following ideas to lavish your volunteers (and church staff members) with love.

1. "This Is Your Life"

For a long-term volunteer, produce a takeoff of the TV show that surprised a guest with people from the past. For example, honor a long-term youth worker, bringing in adults he or she ministered to years earlier to tell how their lives were affected by the leader.

2. Fulfill a secret wish

Another honor for a long-term volunteer is finding out a secret wish that you can fulfill. For example, if a Sunday school teacher who has ministered to hundreds of kids over the past 30 years has always wanted see a Broadway play or take a cruise, your church might fulfill that wish.

3. Provide the right tools

Make a volunteer's job easier by ensuring that he or she has the right equipment. Make sure your volunteer newsletter editor has a decent computer and a top-notch page-layout program. Make sure your Sunday school teachers have the curriculum and supplies they need. Purchase updated equipment for the sound team so they don't have to rig together worn-out equipment each week.

4. Coupon book

This idea allows the people who've been blessed to honor the volunteer who has influenced their lives. The individuals who want to say "thanks" each create a homemade, one-of-a-kind coupon for a service or gift (free babysitting, a home-cooked meal, a car wash, a night at the opera, limousine service to an event) the recipient can redeem.

5. Dinner and a concert

Honor your volunteers with tickets to an event, such as a Christian concert. Ask volunteers to attend as a group. If you can't afford to buy dinner at a restaurant before the concert, hold a potluck at a home before or after the event. This tells your volunteers that you appreciate them and also helps them build bonds with each other. In turn, this will create a stronger volunteer family with less burnout.

6. Hold the presses

Contact a community newspaper editor about the possibility of highlighting a volunteer and his or her service in an article. Or contact the editor of your church's denominational publication or district regional newsletter and suggest a similar feature story.

7. Hold the e-presses

Feature a volunteer on your church Web site. Of course, be careful about what personal information you display online. You can honor a number of volunteers this way, by using several smaller stories or by changing longer stories regularly (monthly or weekly).

8. Personal notes

Purchase a guest book, autograph book, journal, or notebook for each key volunteer. Ask the people they serve to fill the pages with notes of appreciation.

9. Mug 'em

Unexpectedly drop a mug of appreciation by your volunteers' homes. Fill the mug with chocolates or other candies.

10. Happy Birthday

Remember the birthdays of volunteers and staff members. Mail a birthday card signed by the rest of the staff or other volunteers with whom the individual serves. Better yet, make a big fuss of birthdays—everyone likes to have people remember a birthday (as long as you don't remind them how old they are!).

11. Appreciation bulletin

Set up an appreciation board in the church where you can highlight volunteers and staff members. Post a photo of each person in action, and list some interesting facts about the volunteer as well as a couple of words of appreciation from others.

12. Hang banners

Use some creativity and create a simple banner for each volunteer—these can be made from felt and decorated with waterproof markers. Make sure you include a volunteer's name and some specific words of affirmation on each banner. Hang the banners throughout the church. Your volunteers will have fun finding their own banners, and it will create a fun atmosphere your congregation will love.

13. Say it with flowers

Does your church already decorate the auditorium with a bouquet of flowers on the communion table each week? Use the flowers to honor a different volunteer each week, listing the "volunteer of the week" in the bulletin, along with a basic description of how the individual serves the church. Give the honoree the bouquet to take home after the service.

14. Volunteers first

Don't you hate it when you have a church potluck and someone snarfs the best dishes before you get to them? Have the volunteers you're honoring have first crack at the goodies at your next potluck.

15. Street signs

When you have a truly outstanding, long-term volunteer, permanently name a room in the church for that person. Or borrow from what many cities do: In addition to the established names for their streets, the streets might also receive an honorary name for a time. For example, Ash Street might also have a sign noting it as the honorary "Della Lamb Avenue." Be careful not to overuse this one—make sure it's reserved for the truly outstanding, so no one else feels slighted. Another alternative: Each year, you can name rooms in your church after volunteers—during the coming year, room 115 would also be known as "Kurt Smith Study."

16. Dinner on us

If your church offers Wednesday night meals or a coffee cart, occasionally give volunteers a ticket for a free drink or meal. If your church has a bookstore or book rack, give volunteers a standing discount on their purchases.

17. Gift cards

Many restaurants—especially delis and coffee shops—offer gift cards. Even a $5 gift card shows appreciation, especially at a coffee shop. Or buy a gift-certificate book from McDonald's or a local eatery and give individual pages to volunteers.

18. Book 'em

Honor a volunteer and build your church library at the same time. As you purchase new books (or other church members donate them), dedicate the books to volunteers in the church. Place a label in the front of each book that says, "In honor of volunteers service of [Name]" along with the current date. You might even let the volunteer choose one of their favorite resources from a catalog. List new library books and the volunteer each one honors in the bulletin or church newsletter.

19. Details

Gather other information about each volunteer, such as names of children, anniversary date, church anniversary date (when they joined the church or started going there, or began ministering at church). Recruit a volunteer to help you celebrate other key points in each volunteer's life.

20. Book 'em again!

By gathering personal information about volunteers, you can be aware of their interests outside of church; you can then purchase an interesting little book for each volunteer. For example, buy a golfer a book on golf quotes. Many bookstores have bargain racks where you can stock up and still stay within budget.

21. Spiritual gift

Support the spiritual life and growth of volunteers by sending them a portion of Scripture, a devotional booklet, or a Bible in a translation different from the one they generally use.

22. Standouts

Buy something fun that makes all your volunteers stand out. Buy light sticks for all volunteers to wear around their necks or order neon-colored T-shirts for all volunteers in the church. A cool button-down shirt with a ministry logo can make people feel official and special. Encourage other church members to say thanks to these standouts.

23. Pinned

Create and give special pins for volunteers that say something like, "World's Greatest Volunteer" or "I Care. I Volunteer" or "Volunteers Make the World Go 'Round."

24. All expenses paid

If volunteers drive to or chaperone an event as part of their ministry (such as youth workers carpooling kids to a Christian concert), make sure you pay their way!

25. Properly equipped

Make sure volunteers have appropriate training. Often, people burn out because they don't feel equipped for what they're asked to do. Send your youth workers to a convention. Send your newsletter editor to a writers' conference. Send children's workers to a children's ministry conference. If you have a lot of volunteers in a specific area of ministry, schedule training days at your facility.

26. Corny, but sweet

How about giving volunteers a candy bar once in a while with a note attached that says, "You're so sweet to volunteer." Or a candy bar with almonds that says, "We're nuts about you. Thanks for the great job!" Or a $100,000 Bar that says, "You're worth a million!" or "You're grand!" Or a box of Junior Mints and the note "You've mint so much to this church!"

27. It's a date

Give your volunteers a date book at the beginning of each new year. Include a photocopy of the ministry calendar so they can fill in those dates immediately!

28. E-praise

Send frequent praise e-mails, "Hey, I saw you busy in the nursery on Sunday. Those kids sure love you!" This kind of encouragement takes you just a few seconds but will brighten a volunteer's whole day.

29. Payback

Be sure that volunteers get reimbursed for supplies, mileage, or other incidentals. Many won't take advantage of this, believing that providing these items are contributions to the church. But it could be a real blessing for others and free them up to do better (and more) ministry.

30. Memory lane

Make a list of all the people whose lives have been touched by a volunteer. For example, if Greta Jones is celebrating 20 years supervising the church nursery, in addition to giving her a plaque (or her own rocking chair), give her a list of the names of all the babies who've been loved in the nursery during those 20 years.

31. Drive-by appreciation

Show public appreciation for a volunteer by listing his or her name on the church's outdoor sign: "Thanks to our volunteer of the week: John Applebee."

32. Practical needs

Meet the volunteer's personal needs when possible. If an individual is moving into a new house, gather a group of people to help carry boxes and furniture. If the volunteer is dealing with care-giving issues, offer to help in a tangible way. As you serve volunteers, you encourage them to keep serving.

For even more ideas, Group's Church Volunteer Central (www .churchvolunteercentral.com) has a multitude of additional resources including online training to build your volunteers' confidence, certificates you can download and print, and gift items customized for church volunteers. In addition to the numerous articles on motivating and recognizing volunteers on the CVC site, volunteer experts are also available for free telephone consultation, and many more quick practical tips can be found in the archives of the association newsletter, The Inside Track.

28 Tips for Leading Effective Meetings

Meetings—blah! You may cringe just thinking about them, even though—in theory—they serve useful purposes. Use the following ideas to help you end your love-hate relationship with meetings.

Before the Meeting

1. Ask if the meeting is necessary

Meetings serve two purposes: to address issues and reconnect group members. If a meeting involves just a few people or only a couple of topics need discussion, consider meeting via e-mail or phone. The church finance committee might need to meet every month, but the nursery committee might get together only when concerns arise.

2. Check other calendars

Along with calendars for other groups in your church, check local schools, sports, and citywide activity calendars before scheduling your meeting. People are busy, and when they need to make a choice between your meeting or another, attendance suffers for both groups.

3. Set clear beginning and ending times

If people know in advance what kind of time commitment the meeting requires, they'll make more of an effort to attend. Honor this by not going overtime unless you specifically inform everyone of that possibility ahead of time.

4. Provide on-site childcare

Parents might decide not to attend a meeting or function because they don't know what to do with their children. Mention that responsible childcare will be available when you first announce a meeting. Ask parents to let you know if they'll attend the meeting and to provide the names and ages of their children so you can recruit enough volunteers to provide the childcare.

5. Send out agendas a week ahead

Nothing's more frustrating than attending a meeting with no clue of what it's for. E-mail, fax, or snail-mail agendas so attendees can review the topics. At the same time, give people the opportunity to request additions to the agenda.

6. Provide incentives

Don't be afraid to sweeten the pot to increase attendance. To paraphrase a line from a movie: "If you serve it, they will come." Food and drink don't just provide sustenance for meetings. They create an informal atmosphere where participants can experience fellowship and network apart from the agenda. Verbal incentives also encourage people to attend. For example, say, "If we meet now, we won't have to meet again until…" or, "I'm looking forward to covering as many topics as possible at this meeting to cut down on the times we need to meet this year."

7. Combine your meeting time with another event

Gather right after the church service. Or arrange your meeting to end right before the youth group ice-cream social or the choir's spring concert. Just be sure to finish in enough time to move on to the next event.

8. Arrange the room to fit the meeting

If your meeting requires a variety of breakout areas for small groups or video viewing, set up the room with specific sections. Add chairs, bring in tables, and set up audio-visual equipment before others arrive. Set up an area for refreshments, and get coffee, water, or other beverages ready beforehand. If you're serving snacks later in the meeting, prepare the items in advance so you just need to set them out later.

9. Make copies of materials for distribution

Be sure to have extras on hand for people who are able to attend at the last minute. Clearly state if any handouts need to be returned to you before the meeting ends.

During the Meeting

10. Arrive several minutes early

Check the room for any necessary items you might have forgotten. Have pens or pencils and paper handy. Make sure the temperature of the room is comfortable. Add fans or adjust the thermostat if necessary.

11. Welcome everyone individually

Whether your meeting consists of people who've known each other for years or it's a group of "strangers," make an effort to greet each person. Again, you can't do this effectively if you're still running around to finish last-minute preparations.

12. Use name tags

If the meeting involves a standing committee or the people have known each other since childhood, obviously, you can skip the name tags. But if the group is large or those attending aren't familiar with one another, provide blank name tags. Have your name tag on before anyone else walks in. Let those attending make their own so they can use the name they prefer to be called.

13. Start on time

Remember, you've set definite beginning and ending times, and you've printed those on your agenda. Of course, there might be exceptions—if you're waiting for a guest speaker, for example. However, people appreciate a meeting that begins when you say it will.

14. State the rules

This is especially important in meetings where conflict might arise. You don't have to bring a gavel to bang on, but state your expectations. Some examples: "Please stick to the agenda and not divert to other topics"; "Allow others time to speak without interruption"; and "We can have 'healthy' discussions, but let's all avoid making negative personal comments."

15. Address people by name

You don't have to be a dictator when you lead a meeting, but using people's names when they have comments or suggestions allows you to keep control of the meeting's flow without using an iron fist.

16. Be a good listener

What you have to say is important but so are the thoughts and ideas of other participants. Pause after each item on the meeting agenda to make sure everyone understands and has the opportunity to respond.

17. Take time for prayer

You can pray at the start of the meeting, when you break for refreshments, at the end, or you can build in a specific prayer time. But go beyond, "Lord, bless this meeting." These people are part of your church family, so take requests and take time to pray for each other's needs and the overall ministry of your church, in addition to praying for the focus of the group meeting.

18. Aim for consensus

Your group might decide issues that some members don't agree with. Even when you can't get unanimous approval on an issue, you can alleviate feelings of "them against us." Ask all attendees to give their opinions and if they can live with the group's decisions.

19. Realize you don't need all the answers

Most pastors are natural leaders and fall into the trap of giving quick answers. But if you think others have more expertise, let them address issues they understand better than you do. This exchange also allows others to feel more a part of the process and less like observers.

20. Repeat important comments and suggestions

Make sure that people hear and understand what others are saying. For example, say, "What I hear you saying is..." or "How does everyone feel about Judy's comment concerning the need for more classroom space?"

21. Be organized, but flexible

Follow the agenda, but if people have concerns, allow time for comments before moving on. If an issue needs further discussion, suggest that the group consider it again the next time you meet. Offer to meet separately with individuals who bring up issues they think need to be addressed sooner.

RECOMMENDED RESOURCE:

Warm-ups and Wrap-ups: 101 Great Ideas for Small Groups (Group) is a great resource for icebreaker ideas.

22. Keep good notes

Assign a member of the committee or task force to do this. Compile the highlights and send copies to all who attended as well as to people who couldn't make the meeting. Keep a copy on file.

23. Have some fun!

Just because you have to meet doesn't mean you can't enjoy the experience. Get to know one another with an icebreaker activity. If the meeting is long, break the monotony with an activity. For example, break into smaller groups for a brainstorming time to keep everyone active and interested.

24. Keep lecturing to a minimum

Why have a meeting if one person does all the talking? Instead, ask questions and encourage participation—or you might be meeting alone next time!

At the Close

25. Ask for comments about the meeting

Make other meetings better by soliciting feedback. Ask:
- **Was the time we spent on topic valuable?**
- **Did we sufficiently cover the items on the agenda?**
- **Do you think the meeting was a valuable experience?**
- **How could we improve things the next time we meet?**

26. Schedule the next meeting time

Because you're already together, ask people to consult their personal calendars and pencil in the next get-together. Add the time and date to the minutes.

27. Thank everyone for coming

Make sure that participants hear how much you appreciate their comments and suggestions.

28. Remain after the meeting

Stay around for a few minutes in case individuals need to talk with you personally. If a personal discussion seems to be taking too much time, schedule a time to meet and listen to the individual's concerns.

4 Adaptable Meeting Agendas

1. Event-Planning Meetings

1. Open in prayer, keeping the following elements in mind as you pray:

- Wisdom
- Clarity of thought
- Creativity
- Ideas that will meet the needs of those attending the event
- Ideas of ways to draw people to the event
- The volunteers needed for the event
- The impact on people who attend

2. Discuss the purpose behind the event. Don't just assume the event-planning committee knows the reasons your church holds this event.

3. Discuss the goals. Use the following questions:

- How many people do we hope come to the event?
- How do we want this event to impact our church?
- If this is the first time holding this event, do we hope it will be held regularly?

4. Review the history of the event. Ask a committee member to prepare a report on statistics. How many people came? How much did it cost? Was the budget realistic? Also, share the spiritual results of the event. If you received letters or e-mails thanking you for the event or telling what a difference it made, compile those to bless and motivate the committee. In addition, talk through the following practical questions:

- What were the good and bad results?
- What did we learn from last year's event?
- How can we implement those lessons this year?

5. Discuss the logistics of the event. Talk through these points:

- Date. If this is flexible, set it far enough away to allow good planning, but not so far that people lose enthusiasm.
- Cost. Will someone need to make an analysis of this?
- Location. If held at the church, what rooms will be involved, and the logistics of setting up the event, hosting it, and tearing it down.
- Committees needed. If the event is large, you may need to set up committees to work out different details. Who will get these committees together?

- Volunteers. How many do we need? What do we need them to do? How will we recruit them?
- Publicity. How can we best make people aware of this event? Will we need to go beyond announcements at church and in the bulletin? If the event is community-focused, how can we get the word to the community?

6. Conclude the meeting:
- Schedule your next meeting before you leave.
- Make assignments or ask for volunteers to pursue various action items.
- Close in prayer for the event and all the logistics involved.

2. Pastoral Staff-Church Staff Meetings

1. Begin the meeting. Vary how you start so this meeting doesn't become one of those stale weekly meetings. In your introductory comments, take some time to praise different staff members for things you've noticed in their jobs or ministries that week.

2. Lead with a devotional thought. Scriptural topics you might want to focus on:
- Moses' obedience and persistence even when the Israelites didn't follow well (Exodus 14:10-31)
- Joshua's vision and faith (Joshua 1:1-11)
- Eli's laxness (1 Samuel 2:12-36)
- David's respect for others' spiritual authority (1 Samuel 24)
- Nathan's honesty (2 Samuel 12:1-14)
- Solomon's asking God for wisdom to lead his people (1 Kings 3)
- Jonah's reluctance (Jonah 1:1-16)
- Jesus' servant leadership (John 13:1-17)
- Paul's compassion and love for those he served (Acts 20:13-38)

You might want to focus on a leader from the Bible for each meeting, or just at one meeting a month. If you're leading a devotional time for the support staff, choose some biblical characters who were "supporters" to focus on:
- Moses and the ones who held up his arms during battle (Exodus 17:8-13)
- Aaron, Miriam, Joshua and Caleb, as Moses' supporters (Aaron—Exodus 4:10-17; Miriam—Exodus 15:19-21; Joshua and Caleb—Numbers 14:5-9)
- Any of the disciples who supported Jesus (Matthew—Matthew 9:9-13; Peter—Luke 5:1-11; Mark 8:27-29; Thomas—John 11:11-16)

• Barnabas (Acts 9:23-28; 11:22-26)

3. Share an article about ministry, a leadership tip, or a humorous story—something to briefly instruct, inspire, or amuse your staff.

4. Ask each staff member a few personal questions to foster your relationship and the bonding of the group. Or have staff members form pairs to ask questions of each other.

5. Invite each staff member to briefly tell the others something he or she has learned from Scripture the past week.

6. Discuss details of upcoming worship services. Let those involved in services share necessary details. Provide an order of service for each staff member to browse.

7. Discuss details of other upcoming events. Double-check and make sure everyone knows their responsibilities, and check to see if anyone needs help from the others.

8. Ask each staff member to give a five-minute update on his or her area of ministry. Staff members can bring up issues for discussion during this time, or they can go into more detail later. Be sure to praise individual staff members and acknowledge and reaffirm their gifts. As staff members share, encourage them to focus more on how their ministries are affecting and changing people and less on facts and numbers.

9. Discuss any other meetings you need to schedule beyond the regular staff meeting, such as a budget-review meeting or a meeting to plan an event.

10. Close the meeting by discussing assignments for that week or for the next meeting.

11. Spend time in prayer. Pray around the group or ask for volunteers to pray about each item brought up during the meeting. In addition to praying for each other, focus on one or more of these elements during your prayer time:

- Wisdom for leadership
- Encouragement for the challenges of ministry
- Patience for issues involving difficult people
- Praise for being a part of ministry and serving God
- Thanksgiving for the team God has put together
- God's guidance for directing souls and ministries
- Compassion and a shepherd's heart

Additional tips for success:

- **Keep the beginning of the meeting brief.** If you give a devotional thought, such as focusing on leaders, keep it as brief as possible. Remember this isn't a sermon or workshop. If what you share provokes discussion, that's OK for a few minutes. But limit that discussion time or your whole staff meeting agenda will be blown.
- **Be sensitive to the Holy Spirit's leading.** It's good to keep the meeting moving, but if staff members need to discuss something in depth and another issue can wait a week, be flexible.
- **Encourage *some* chatting.** Your staff needs to chat to blow off steam, release tension, and build the bonds between them. A team that connects personally as well as professionally or in ministry will be most successful.
- **Encourage staff members to prepare for the meeting.** If they have concerns to discuss, urge them to let you know ahead of time so you can plan adequate time to cover these issues.
- **Heap praise on your staff members during meetings.** Be specific. Affirm them when they use their spiritual gifts, natural skills, and even when they step out of their comfort zones. However, save reprimands and corrections for private meetings.

3. Committee Meetings

1. Begin the meeting with inspiration, encouragement, or appreciation. Most committees are comprised of volunteers led by a staff member, so use every opportunity to feed their souls, stoke their desire to make a difference, sharpen their vision, and even to appropriately boost their egos and sense of self-worth. Take special care to bless your volunteers, choosing from these ideas:

- Begin with prayer. Thank God for bringing together these team members.
- Praise the group for the fine job they're doing with their ministry. Where possible, be specific.
- Relate "feel-good" anecdotes about the ministry this committee guides. For example, share a note from someone who was blessed by the ministry.
- Ask someone from the congregation to attend the meeting and express how he or she has been blessed by the ministry.
- Lead with a devotional thought.
- Read a Scripture passage that will inspire the committee members.

- Share an article, a leadership tip, statistics, or a humorous story that specifically ties in with this ministry.
- Remind people of the purpose and importance of the ministry this committee guides.
- Introduce any new members.

2. Provide an update on the logistics of the ministry. This might include attendance figures, budget concerns, equipment issues, or supply needs. Spend time discussing ideas to resolve any problems you're facing logistically.

3. Provide an update on the spiritual aspects of the ministry. This might include additional stories of how people have been affected by the ministry, commitments that people have made, or other recent successes or challenges the ministry has had.

4. Discuss results of any goals or action items set at the previous meeting.

5. Go around the room and ask committee members for an update on their specific areas of responsibility.

6. Discuss new items, such as training opportunities coming up or the need to look into new equipment or supplies.

7. Mention long-term plans or goals that the committee needs to be working on.

8. Close by making assignments on action items or by setting goals for what the group needs to accomplish before the next meeting.

4. New Ministry Start-up Meetings

1. Begin the meeting by praying briefly, or by sharing a short devotional thought.

2. Go around the room so each member can introduce himself or herself. As the leader, you should carry this along. If some of these people have not met each other before or don't know much about each other, ask them to tell a bit about their personal lives. If they do know each other fairly well, encourage people to tell why they're interested in serving on this committee or why the new ministry is important to them.

3. Cast the vision. Tell the group your personal hopes and dreams for the ministry this team will be starting. Allow time for others to talk about their dreams for the ministry.

4. Tell committee members what the team needs to accomplish. Outline different jobs available and the time commitments for these responsibilities. Encourage people to volunteer for specific jobs not just because a need exists, but because it is something they'll enjoy and feel rewarded by doing.

5. Make sure people know what's expected of them—not only for this committee or volunteer responsibility, but as church leaders in general. As they take on their roles in the church, what expectations does the church have for these leaders?

6. Invite committee members to ask questions.

7. Ask people to volunteer for specific roles in this ministry. Also encourage people to pray about their involvement before volunteering.

8. Have committee members fill out a contact-information form before they leave. Technology rules, so be sure to get cell phone numbers and e-mail addresses.

9. Set a time for the next meeting, when the committee will get into the hard work of planning the ministry.

10. Close the meeting in prayer. Thank God for the people serving on the committee, and ask God to help you all find your places and glorify him through this new ministry.

13 Creative Ways to Train Leaders and Volunteers

Imagine that you schedule a workshop and *everyone* shows up! Imagine further that they show up because they know they'll experience new ideas, receive valuable information, and learn creative hands-on ways to work within their ministries. Wow!

How would you like to have a reputation for offering fresh and exciting workshops? You can! The following ideas will help you have some fun, pass along useful information, and build a stronger ministry team.

1. Use modern technology

Tap into the Internet for Web sites with ideas for training, interactive games to play during training, and certificate downloads. Search for information on specific topics, such as *"outreach ideas that really work."* E-mail friends and associates for advice. Use e-card invites to invite people to the training.

2. Step out of the adult box

Adults enjoy a snappy beginning as much as children. Start with a fun activity to promote team building. Arrange your participants in a circle—or if the group is large, several small circles of seven to eight participants each. Provide one rope for each circle, and have each person hold on with both hands. Now, either using blindfolds or having everyone close their eyes, instruct each group to form a square. The group members are allowed to talk, but not look. Let the groups work through this for three or four minutes. They'll quickly discover that to accomplish this task, they must work together, listen to another (even the introverts), and talk through each step to make the square. If they want to try again, repeat the exercise with another geometric shape!

3. Pass the expertise

Bring in experts to teach portions of the training. Check with other local churches or nonprofit organizations for suggestions of people who can speak on subjects related to your workshop. For example, train everyone on a new church-data program by taking advantage of the representatives from the company selling the program. For facility fundamentals—such as the operation of temperature-control centers, evacuation plans for emergencies, or location of stepladders and tools—ask your facilities manager (or the layperson who functions as the building manager) to provide a tour of the church. Bring in an adult with a disability to help children's teachers understand the challenges disabled children face.

4. Show what *not* to do

Without telling the participants, spend the first five minutes of the training doing everything you shouldn't do. Arrive late to your own meeting, don't have anything prepared, forget materials or people's names. Then stop the charade and ask the group what you did wrong. Make a list of the don'ts. For each "don't," take suggestions about how a task should be done.

5. Use skits

Present a Bible story, such as the prodigal son, and ask participants to divide into small groups. Instruct the smaller groups to prepare a skit for the whole group portraying the story in modern times. You can tell them to only use props they can find in the room or you can provide a box of items. Allow about 15 minutes for the groups to create their skits, and then present the skits for each other. This not only builds teamwork, but also gives participants a unique tool to use during training times in their own ministries throughout the year.

6. Use a theme

Choose a recent movie, play, or book familiar to most of the participants. For example, the family film *Because of Winn-Dixie* demonstrates an important ministry lesson: the influence one person has in many other lives. Design your workshop around the movie theme. Set up your room like a *neighborhood,* complete with facades of cutout houses and picket fences (all made from cardboard). Each home might represent different types of people the church or program area will minister to throughout the year (such as two-parent families, single-parent homes, blended families, or families facing divorce). Guide participants through the neighborhood. At each home provide information on specific challenges each kind of family faces. Provide questions to think about and discuss. In the case of divorce, for example, how can you make it easier for children to be involved in activities when they live in two different homes? Come together at the end, and discuss the ideas participants come up with. Close by providing a picnic lunch (as in the movie) so that people can get to know one another better.

7. Divide participants into senior and new members

Pair your church "veterans" with newbies. If you're short on veterans, create small groups of newbies along with a senior leader to facilitate each group. Provide senior members with a list of questions related to your workshop. Allow a specific amount of time for pairs or groups to discuss the questions. Afterward, draw everyone together and with a chalkboard or flip chart handy, list all the suggestions that groups brainstormed for each topic.

8. Invite everyone to a theater experience

Decorate the training or workshop room with muted lighting, a fake curtain, exit signs, and posters of movies. Arrange chairs in theater seating. If you're tech-savvy, use PowerPoint so participants can watch and learn while they're waiting for the show to begin. Throw in trivia questions like "How many children participated in the Sunday school program this year?" or "How many pounds of food did we provide for the homeless last month?" Flash the answers after a few seconds. Have a concession stand for your refreshment area with popcorn, sodas, and candy. Give each participant a ticket as he or she enters. Use background music as people move through the workshop. Play "Whistle While You Work" from Disney's *Snow White and the Seven Dwarfs* to signal when small discussion groups should start and end. End the whole meeting with "Day by Day" from *Godspell.*

9. Board Noah's ark

This works well for almost any workshop, and it gets creative juices flowing! Move outdoors if weather permits. Decorate the meeting area with streamers in rainbow colors. Instruct participants to come "on board," two by two. When all are seated, ask them to think about the conditions that Noah and his family faced living on the ark (boredom, crowded quarters, sanitation, food). Then ask participants how they think Noah and his family dealt with these issues, and list all the possibilities on a flip chart. Finally, ask participants to reflect upon conditions that exist in the church or within their ministry areas that need help or revamping. Spend time taking ideas from participants, looking for ways to resolve problems.

10. Gather in a cozy atmosphere

For a unique and relaxing environment, conduct your training in a restaurant, at a park, or in your own home. Sometimes a change in scenery increases attendance and provides a more memorable workshop experience. Many restaurants offer private rooms. Parks often have shelter houses that can be reserved for little or no cost. Using your own home allows you to divide participants into smaller groups and separate rooms with little effort.

11. Tools of the trade

If you're leading a workshop with mostly new people, set up your area like a woodworking shop. Scatter some sawdust on the floor (of course, be careful that no one slips), dress in overalls, and place caution tape across the entryway. Arrange enough tables so all participants can gather in small groups. On each table place a variety of woodworking tools. Invite people to sit down, welcome them to the construction site, and tell them they've been assigned to a special ministry job. Before them lie the tools of their trade.

Once the laughter subsides, tell each group to make a list of all the items on their tables. Next to each item, write a sentence about how a specific tool might help participants remember an important part of their ministry. For example, a hammer might remind them of growing the ministry. A measuring tape might represent how far leaders have brought their ministries and how far they can still go. A saw might suggest sharpening the focus of the ministry or cutting back on waste. Come back together and go over each small group's answers.

12. Road trip

Plan time away from the church for training. Check into a retreat house or ask someone in the church if you can borrow a lake house or cabin for a retreat. Getting away from it all allows everyone to jump into the training faster without distractions, phone calls, and responsibilities present in the church building.

13. Try lesson training

Send participants invitations to join you for Sunday school, youth group, or a family activity, depending upon what training you're offering. Lead the ministry just like it would occur. For example, for Sunday school teacher training, meet teachers at the door as if they were students, ask them their names, and have them make name tags. They can sit at the type of table and chairs the students in their classes use. Cover a complete lesson with breaks, activities, and snacks. Signal the end of the session and ask participants to write on a whiteboard or flipchart one important lesson they learned from the exercise. Then discuss the responses.

12 Ways to Identify and Encourage Leaders

You've probably felt the pressure of finding lay leaders for specific areas of ministry. The good news is that people want to be involved in serving God in leadership roles, and the Lord has placed potential leaders in your midst. The following ideas can help you discover lay leaders for ministry in your church.

1. Cultivate a strong biblical philosophy

Start by creating a church culture that calls people to serve the Lord humbly. That begins with you and other paid staff members. When a church is small and just getting started, everyone helps. However, when a church grows, it adds staff and depends on lay leaders less and less. No matter how small or large your church is now, work to recapture the spirit of the new church.

2. Communicate needs

If people can't see a need, they won't feel compelled to lead. In addition, make sure you're not holding people back because they see you trying to do everything yourself. Instead, actively practice the art of involving others.

3. Lead by example

As pastor, you're the pacesetter for your church and its ministries. Your example is crucial. Your standards, commitment, and quality of leadership provide powerful examples to those you serve. Consider these qualities of a strong leader, evaluating whether you demonstrate them and whether you've observed them in others in your church:

- A Christlike leader walks ahead of the group without being detached from the group.
- A strong leader is authentic.
- An effective leader not only listens well, but knows how to respond to differences and even to criticism.
- A great leader senses the pulse of the group and earns respect over time.
- A successful leader leads with clear thinking, not emotions.
- A dedicated leader follows through on details.
- A God-honoring leader is a person of prayer.

4. Involve everyone in some way

Of course, not everyone will lead a ministry. But in a sense, every volunteer is a leader. Also, you can't identify potential ministry leaders if people aren't serving at all. Follow the advice in the simple adage: "Use me or lose me." Everyone in your church can do something. Encourage reluctant servants to consider the prayer, "I am only one, but I am one; I cannot do everything, but I can do something. What I can do, I ought to do, and what I ought to do, by God's grace I will do."

5. Begin with one person

As you seek out leaders, find one individual to pray with and for. Mentor this individual. Help him or her understand the importance of serving. This person will connect with others, and they'll eventually become a team.

6. Know who can do what

Help people find their niches. Don't force round pegs into square holes. Some leaders will have gifts for organization and administration, while others will be equipped to meet people's spiritual needs. Be aware of the interests and skills of the key people you're mentoring, and you can help them plug in to lead where they fit best.

7. Plan at least one retreat a year

Gather all volunteers together for prayer, celebration, affirmation, and encouragement. You might be surprised at how God works in one retreat experience to bolster the ranks of church leaders.

8. Ask current leaders to share insights

When existing leaders talk about what they've gained while serving the Lord in particular ministry areas, they encourage potential leaders to take the next step. Encourage them to share what they've learned with others.

9. Be real

Show brief video testimonials during a worship service, or print written versions in your bulletin or newsletter. When people hear both the challenges and the good things happening in ministry, they'll be more willing to step up and take leadership roles.

10. Have volunteers choose leaders

Ask current volunteers in an area of ministry to pray for and make suggestions about who should lead them. It's easier to discover leaders when the group they'll be leading chooses them.

11. Have a plan and purpose

If you want new leaders to have good experiences, you need to prepare carefully, develop a clear purpose, and provide leadership. Proceed slowly, prayerfully, and methodically. Constantly remind leaders that they're serving God and that what they're doing should glorify him.

12. Develop good ministry descriptions for leaders

Make sure potential leaders know exactly what's expected of them—as well as what's not expected. Provide good resources and good communication for the ministries you've asked them to lead.

To get even more ideas for building up your leaders and volunteers, be sure to check out Group's Church Volunteer Central (www .churchvolunteercentral.com), a virtual treasure-trove of articles, online training resources, and other useful tools that will help you to recruit, equip, retain, and lead your church volunteers.

Section 8:
Community Service and Outreach

Reaching outside the walls of the church is vital for the health of any church. Why? Think about the Dead Sea: Although the Jordan river flows into it, there is no outlet, causing stagnation. The same can happen to your church. The ideas in this section will help your congregation reach out both locally and around the world. The result will be streams of people coming in and going out, ensuring that your church remains growing and alive.

Section 8: Table of Contents

18 Service Projects

How can you best reach out to the people around you? Someone once said, "People don't care how much you know until they know how much you care." Nothing tells a community "We care!" more than discovering and meeting their needs. The following church-tested service projects allow you to show your community just how much your church cares.

1. Keep it clean

Crossroads Church of the Nazarene in Ellicott City, Maryland, adopted a mile of local highway that volunteers make sure remains trash-free. A sign marks the church's stretch of the road and gives credit for its work. Of course, this makes local residents aware of the church and its service spirit! A church near Seattle serves its community by cleaning up a state park.

Check with your local or state highway department about keeping a stretch of road beautiful. Or contact the local parks department to volunteer by painting and repairing local playgrounds, tending to grounds, or picking up trash.

2. Teen power

Teens from a church in Indianapolis discovered a great way to serve their community. They surveyed local neighborhoods and noted houses needing yardwork. They then went door to door offering to mow lawns, clean up yards, and trim bushes. They ended up praying with some of the people they served and also took many opportunities to invite people to church.

Most teens like grittiness and reality—even if they might not want to work up a sweat. However, with a yardwork project like this, the teens in your church could get excited about making a real difference in people's lives.

3. Community celebrations

Every year, Independence, Missouri, holds a Labor Day celebration called Santa Caligon. It takes place where the Santa Fe, California, and Oregon Trails intersected to take settlers west in the 1800s. The city blocks off a couple of square miles of the old downtown to hold street-festival events. Because the Labor Day weekend usually comes with temperatures in the 90s, several local churches rent booths and use the opportunity to pass out free cups of cold water.

What festivals take place locally in your area? See if they offer reduced rates to nonprofit organizations for booths or display tables.

4. Batteries included

First Baptist Church in Greenwood, Missouri, conducts a "battery ministry." Church members donate 9-volt batteries, and teams from the church go door to door, offering fresh batteries for smoke detectors—along with information about their church.

5. Banking basics

What special skills do the people in your church have that could lend themselves to a service project? One church with a number of accountants as members offers a finance ministry. Volunteers help people with training and hands-on practice in areas such as balancing a checkbook, creating a plan for getting out of debt, and teaching how to create budgets. In a Philadelphia church offering this ministry, leaders "take over" a family's checkbook for a while—helping them write checks and approving all purchases while the family is enrolled in the program.

6. Med squad

One church with a number of doctors, nurses, and other medical personnel in its congregation sends out a medical team when natural disasters strike. The church also involves its community by soliciting donations that go directly to the disaster victims—a great opportunity to show the community that the church cares.

7. Auto and home

Another church offers an oil change and general car checkup ministry in its community. The same idea works if your church has a number of people with construction or handyman skills. Build a construction-team ministry to help local residents with minor home repairs.

10 SCHOOL SERVICE PROJECTS:

If you'd like to focus your church's service projects on local schools, consider these "bonus" ideas.

1. Create an after-school "club" at your church for youth in the area. Make it a safe place where kids can come and hang out. If your facility has a gym, create an after-school basketball league. Or get the kids in your church involved in creating a skaters' park on the edge of the church parking lot.

2. Provide tutoring for students. Schedule the tutoring at the church so that any adult volunteer and the child being tutored are never alone together, and follow the local district's policy (or your church's, if it's stricter) for background checks on adults working with children.

3. Help with fundraising. Some schools collect Campbell's soup and other product labels for education (www.labelsforeducation.com) or Box Tops for Education (www.boxtops4education .com). Others collect aluminum cans, hold silent auctions, or sponsor special events.

4. Start a breakfast program for community kids, serving a hot meal one or more times each week.

5. Institute a mentoring or big brother/big sister program.

6. Partner with school officials to conduct a special class to train kids to be peer-mediators at school.

7. Host a Moms in Touch group (www.momsintouch.org) at your church, praying for students and staff at schools in your area and supporting school officials in practical ways.

8. Keep an eye on the school calendar as the academic year progresses, identifying teacher workdays when kids will be out of school, and provide special programs during those times. You might adapt VBS curriculum, but for just a day or two at a time.

9. Set up a computer lab at your church for students who don't have access to current computers or supplies.

10. Adopt the teachers in your congregation, and see how you can support them as the year progresses.

8. S.O.S.: Serve Our Schools

What if you could give a local school district thousands of dollars worth of service? Pleasant Valley Baptist Church in Liberty, Missouri, did just that! When a local district faced budget cuts and financial crisis, the church looked for a way to help. Members tackled repainting/renovation projects the school district had planned but couldn't afford.

The first year, the church saved the school district $25,000 in labor costs by gathering people to work on an elementary school that needed updating. The second year, the church joined forces with two other local outreach-oriented churches and saved the district $40,000 by doing summer renovations.

Pleasant Valley also opens the church doors for the school district to hold teacher-training events in its large facilities. Church members also gather school supplies for families who can't afford them. By partnering with the local school district, the church has become a familiar ground for the 28 schools in the district and their more than 17,000 students.

Keep an eye on school districts in your area, and volunteer as needs arise. Or meet with school officials to let them know your church wants to serve local schools—with no strings attached.

9. A place for the homeless

About 50 churches in Dane County, Wisconsin, participate in the Interfaith Hospitality Network to provide overnight lodging and meals to homeless families. Guests stay in the designated church for a week at a time. Church volunteers support families by providing meals and hosting the guests.

If your church has a gym shower and a place to set up cots, you could be a blessing to a family that's down and out.

10. Reap what you sew

The knitting group at one church has a unique outreach. They knit gloves and scarves for children and others in need. Other churches have quilting groups. Members enjoy fellowship while they create quilts to donate to crisis-pregnancy centers, hospitals, and other service centers in their communities.

11. Second-hand deals

St. John's Episcopal Church in Chevy Chase, Maryland, has served its community since 1951 by operating a recycle store called the Opportunity Shop. The store provides bargains for people in the community, and the proceeds go to support a community ministry.

Can't run a thrift store? Host a huge garage sale to raise money for community organizations.

12. Fundraising support

North Coast Church members in Vista, California, serve a local organization that houses people with HIV/AIDS. Members sign up to take residents out of the house and treat them to a movie or other local event. The church also helps raise money for the residence through fundraisers. One is called "stroll by the sea"—church members sign up to walk and also volunteer for setup and tear down.

Members of your church might not have a sea to stroll by, but perhaps they can walk as a group at a community fundraiser, sponsor a drink table, or volunteer for the cleanup crew.

13. Food drive

One local church partners with a food pantry to hold drives four times a year. In addition, if the pantry runs short between the regular drives, leaders send an SOS to the church. On a designated Sunday, church members bring grocery bags of food and leave them on the trunks of their cars when they arrive for church. Trucks from the community pantry make the rounds through the parking lot, picking up the food while church members worship inside.

If your community doesn't have a food pantry, provide grocery items and prepaid gift cards or gift certificates to local supermarkets.

14. Caregiver relief

Lutheran Church of the Resurrection in Marietta, Georgia, offers practical help to people with developmental disabilities such as mental retardation, cerebral palsy, and autism.

Even if your church can't help individuals with disabilities learn new skills, check into providing help to family members, where volunteers stay with the developmentally disabled person while the caregivers get shopping done, run errands, or just get a break to go out to dinner or see a movie.

15. Expanded children's ministry

In addition to offering a children's ministry, some churches discover other ways to minister to families with children. Some offer a parents' day out to give Mom or Dad a break. Others host large community events, such as carnivals featuring giant inflatable slides, tunnels, and moonwalks, as well as crafts, petting zoos, clowns, and face-painting.

16. Seniors ministry

On the other end of the spectrum, consider helping your community with a senior-services ministry. This can be as simple as teams volunteering at a local nursing home. Or your congregation can make a more dramatic difference by getting involved in helping seniors get to doctor appointments, delivering meals to their homes, or doing anything else that helps seniors maintain their independence.

17. Grocery payback

St. John's Episcopal Church in Chevy Chase, Maryland, partners with a local grocery-store chain. With regular grocery shopping, people from the church members support the community. Members purchase grocery gift cards at the church and use them "same as cash" at full value at the store. In return for the business, the grocery chain donates a portion from the sale of each card to St. John's Outreach, including the church's program to help feed the homeless, clothe and shelter the poor, and care for the infirm.

18. Trash cash

Some churches promote recycling with garage sale or resale shop ministries, but have you considered serving the community by setting up a recycling program? Even if your community doesn't require residents to recycle paper, glass, metal, and plastic products, reducing trash is an issue that probably concerns many community members. Organize a recycling program, designate your church as the drop-off point, and advertise the program from door to door. You can create business-card-sized magnets, using sheets you can run through your computer's printer; community residents can put them on their refrigerators to remind them that you take items to be recycled. Extend your ministry by using profits from the recycling program to support other community services.

12 Outreach Ideas

Many pastors and their churches have discovered new and untraveled ways to reach out to their communities. With these unique strategies in hand, they bring in many new visitors who go on to become contributing and committed members of their congregations. What are some of those methods, and how do you use them to great effect in your own community?

Educate Yourself

Constantly be looking for new ideas. Adopt and adapt until the ideas fit your church. Some ways to stay abreast of the latest and greatest:

1. Read

Without digging too deep, you'll quickly find a number of publications, Web sites, books, and other resources geared specifically to outreach and ministry. Start with an online search, using terms such as "outreach" or "evangelism"; add a word like "magazine" or "book" to your search to get more specific results. Set aside part of your church's outreach budget to purchase books and subscribe to magazines or membership Web sites. Create an outreach library to share these resources.

2. Study local newspapers

Churches typically place ads in local newspapers to draw people to outreach-oriented events. Check the religion or faith section of your daily newspaper; many newspapers print these sections each Saturday. You're likely to find both ads and feature articles pertaining to outreach events. You'll keep up with what's going on your community, plus generate ideas that might be worth adapting for your own church.

3. Encourage your congregation to search for good ideas

You don't have to do all the legwork. Simply let your congregation know that they should pass along any outreach-growth ideas they hear of. Question staff and lay leaders when they return from workshops and conferences. Ask what they found fresh or upbeat while traveling.

4. Go to conferences

Workshops for church leaders, worship leaders, and pastors offer all kinds of material from some of the best people in the field. Attend conferences with the goal of gathering ideas. It can be easy to retreat during conferences, but take opportunities to chat informally with other pastors—finding that one successful outreach that another church has already accomplished successfully might be worth the entire cost of attending a conference.

Church Growth Ideas

The following ideas can specifically help you "do" outreach that brings new people into your church.

5. Offer support/recovery groups

Be clear that these groups aren't just for the people of your church, but for anyone facing these problems. Some support groups you might want to consider include the following:

- MOPS (Mothers of Preschoolers)
- AA (Alcoholics Anonymous), or AL-ANON for those who have family members struggling with alcohol dependency or abuse
- Parenting groups
- Premarriage/marriage counseling groups
- Toastmasters (for people who want to speak more effectively)
- Drug-dependency groups
- Addiction-recovery groups
- Grief-recovery groups
- Groups addressing homosexuality issues (parent support, HIV/AIDS counseling)
- Job-seeker groups (to assist people with résumés, finding jobs, and other networking)
- Anger management and other emotional problems
- Domestic abuse
- Stepfamilies and blended families
- Divorce recovery
- Alzheimer's patients and caregivers

RECOMMENDED RESOURCE:
For more detailed information on top outreach ideas, check out *Group's Body-Building Guide to OUTREACH*.

GROUP'S BODY-BUILDING GUIDE TO
OUTREACH
★★★★★
STRETCHING
OUT
TO YOUR
COMMUNITY

As you create support groups for these and other problems, be sure to offer support from wide-ranging psychological and medical disciplines in addition to biblical support. While outreach and ministry are the focus for these groups, make the support angle top priority. Offer appropriate support and help even if attendees aren't immediately interested in finding a church home.

6. Sponsor rallies

Some churches offer once-a-year car rallies, where both church members and community people can put antique or "specialty" cars on display in the parking lot for a day of fun and camaraderie. You could sponsor other kinds of rallies, depending on your congregation's and community's interests, including motorcycle groups and clubs, women's crafts and hobbies, or collectors' interests (coins, stamps, autographs). By opening your facility for rallies, you'll make people aware that your church is a happening place.

7. Conferences

Weekend conferences and workshops will draw people from your community. Consider holding a local writers' conference, a back-to-school conference for teachers and administrators, or a youth conference for teenagers or for local agencies that work with youth.

8. Times and seasons

Sponsor an event such as a "Living Christmas Tree" concert at Christmas, a Passion play at Easter, or a Patriot's Weekend around July 4. Simply connect your events to holidays. Hold a festival that offers an alternative for Halloween (see www.group.com/heroes for a great Halloween alternative outreach program) or a Valentine's Day banquet, in addition to the more typical events at Christmas and Easter.

9. Coffeehouse and meeting rooms

Open a coffee bar in your facility and let people in the community know that local groups can use rooms for meetings. Word will spread that you have an open, inquiring, and embracing congregation. Talk to organizers of community-education programs in your area and offer your church as a meeting place.

10. Blood drives and community health projects

Even if you can't organize these events yourself, you can provide space in your facility for organizations that already offer these services. In exchange for use of your building, the organizers just need to let you display brochures and information about your church and its ministries.

11. Polling place

Volunteer your church as a polling place during election seasons. While voting rules might limit what direct contact you can have with voters, it still portrays your church as an accessible place where people care about the community.

12. Parents' day out

Have volunteers from your church watch and teach young children while their parents get a needed break. With this event, you'll definitely make solid connections with parents in your community.

Be sure to provide background checks for anyone who works with children, and find out if church policy is adequate. A very useful resource is Group's Church Volunteer Central network (churchvolunteercentral.com), which offers ready-made background-check and parental-consent forms, as well as articles, online training resources, and many other useful tools to help recruit, equip, retain, and lead church volunteers.

13 Ways to Involve Your Church in World Missions

If your church holds an annual missions conference or gives some regular services a missions emphasis, you already know how great it is to get your church family "pumped up" about global missions. The problem is what to do the rest of the year! How can you help members of your congregation live with a world-missions mind-set? What steps can you take to develop a passion for global outreach in the heart of your church? The following ideas can help your congregation understand the importance of missions and take practical steps to get more involved.

1. Go there

Send people overseas. When church-family members participate in short-term mission trips and interact with missionaries in other countries, they see needs firsthand and almost naturally develop an infectious passion to reach that part of the world. Equip and empower people who've returned from mission trips to share their excitement with others in the congregation. During worship services, interview returning church members about their trips. If your church has the technology, show a few minutes of still photos or video of the trip. Focus on the faces of the people they went to serve. Or ask your short-termers to lead an adult Sunday school class or write reflections about their trip for the church newsletter, bulletin, or Web site.

2. The world glowing with prayer

Infuse enthusiasm for world missions into your congregation with this family-based activity. Post a large black-and-white map of the world in your church foyer and place a bucket filled with various fluorescent highlighters on the floor below it. Explain that each week, families should look at the map together and select a country they'll commit to pray for together each day of the upcoming week. When they've chosen a country, a family member should grab a highlighter and color in the selected country.

Challenge families to learn more about their chosen countries during the week, focusing especially on any crises in that country (war, poverty, persecution, dictatorship, natural disasters); on the spiritual needs of the people there; and on the efforts of missionaries serving there. Make copies of specific information on missionaries your church supports available to families. Direct them to the sites listed in the sidebar on page 212, "8 Great Web Sites for Finding World Missions Information," where they can learn more about unreached people groups around the globe.

Prompt families to select and color in a new country each week. If possible, set up a black light so that it shines on the map to make the fluorescent highlighter colors glow. Eventually, through the combined efforts of everyone in your church, every country on the map will be colored in—and covered in prayer. Then put up a new map and start the exercise again!

3. Sunday morning spotlight

Shine a spotlight on missions every chance you get! Incorporate one missions-oriented element in every main worship service. Share a fact about a country that needs missionaries (again, see the sidebar "8 Great Web Sites for Finding World Missions Information"), pray for a missionary family by name during the service, and print the Web address of a mission-focused Web site in your bulletin each week.

4. Make missions giving fun

One of the most important ways your church can support global ministries is to give financially to missionaries and ministry organizations. Instead of just "passing the plate," create unique and fun ways for your church family to give to missions. A few suggestions:

- Implement a churchwide garage sale and give proceeds directly to missions work.
- Organize a penny drive for young children, challenging them to give loose change. Ask Sunday school teachers to share the story of the poor widow's offering (Mark 12:41-44) as they invite kids to bring coins to give in a special offering.
- Host a community run or mini-marathon and ask participants to solicit pledges. Focus on a ministry organization that addresses a global need that will interest both Christians and non-Christians in your community, such as famine and poverty relief, AIDS or other medical needs, orphans, or natural disaster recovery.

8 Great Web Sites for Finding
World Missions Information

1. www.joshuaproject.net

Focuses on people groups, highlighting the groups of the world that have the least Christian presence.

2. www.gmi.org/ow

Highlights the prayer needs of various countries. Also includes a link asking prayer for "countries in crisis."

3. www.missionaryresources.org

Provides missionaries and other users with articles, links, books, videos, and discussions on a wide variety of missions topics.

4. www.mnnonline.org

Keeps Christians informed of mission activity around the world, with the goal of motivating Christians to prayer, participation, and support of missionary work.

5. www.imb.org/WE/pplink.asp

Assists churches in taking an active and direct role in missions by adopting an unreached people group.

6. www.ksafe.com/profiles/home.html

Offers profiles of more than 1,600 unreached people groups.

7. www.urbana.org

Provides college students and young adults with information about global missions and challenges them with the world's needs.

8. www.uscwm.org

Focuses on ensuring that distinct people groups of the world are "reached," and offers shared solutions to common obstacles in mission efforts.

5. God's heart for the world in the Word

The Bible is full of Scripture passages that communicate God's love for all the nations. Include reading one of these passages aloud as part of your regular worship services. As the people of your church hear about God's passion for all people groups each week, their passion for the world will increase. If individuals in your church speak other languages, invite them to read Scripture in their native tongue for the congregation, followed by the English version. The following Scripture passages work well:

- Psalm 22:27-31; 67:1-7; 72:17
- Malachi 1:11
- Matthew 28:18-20
- Romans 16:25-27
- Galatians 3:25-29
- Revelation 5:9-10; 7:9-10

6. Fast for famine

Did you know that 30,000 children around the world die each day due to poverty or hunger-related diseases? Challenge members of your congregation to join you in fasting for at least one meal during the upcoming week. Instead of eating, participants should spend time praying for those who are poor and hungry around the world as well as praying for missionaries working to provide food and shelter for people in need. Invite those who give up a meal to estimate the amount of money they would have spent and donate it to a ministry or aid agency focused on world hunger.

7. My missionary hero

Help young people get excited about missions, and empower them to inspire their church family. Recruit interested preteen and teenage students to read biographies of missionaries. Stories of people from early church history (St. Patrick) as well as more recent centuries (Hudson Taylor, Amy Carmichael, Jim and Elisabeth Elliot, Bruce Olson, David Livingstone, Martin and Gracia Burnham) are exciting and inspiring! Check with your local Christian bookstore or an online bookstore to order copies of books like the Trailblazers Books (Bethany House) by Dave and Neta Jackson for younger readers. Or purchase copies of *End of the Spear* (Tyndale, 2005) by Steve Saint (which was released as a motion picture in early 2006), *In the Presence of My Enemies* (Tyndale, 2004) by Gracia Burnham, or the classic *Bruchko* by Bruce Olson (YWAM, 2005) for teenagers.

When a child or teenager finishes reading a missionary biography, invite him or her to give a short presentation to the church during a Sunday morning service, telling the story of that missionary's life. Also, encourage readers to tell the congregation one way the missionary's life has inspired them personally.

8. Missionary mirror

Help the people of your church see themselves as missionaries. Create a portrait wall in your church foyer featuring framed photographs of missionaries your church supports. Under each portrait, include a small card that lists the missionaries' names and where they serve. Somewhere in the middle of the portrait wall, hang up a framed mirror. Under the mirror, post a card with this text: "*You* are a missionary. Your mission field: *Everywhere* you go."

9. God's globe, God's love

Equip Sunday school teachers of upper-elementary-aged students to coordinate a craft that can be used to celebrate global missions. Sunday school classes will need two weeks to make this craft. Kids will require the following supplies: balloons (one per child), newspaper strips, papier-mâché mix (available at craft stores), masking tape, fishing wire (or string), tempera paints of various colors, and a globe or map of the world.

The first week, teachers should help children create papier-mâché "globes" using balloons as the basic shape. The following Sunday, after the papier-mâché has dried, children can pop the balloons. Teachers should use masking tape to affix long strings of fishing wire on the end of each sphere. Kids can then paint their creations to look like globes, depicting the continents and countries of the earth.

When the globes have dried, recruit assistants to help you hang the globes from the ceiling of your church foyer or worship area. Mention them during a worship service, thanking the children for reminding the church family of God's love for all the nations and peoples of the earth.

10. Music of many languages

Help your congregation feel united with Christians around the globe by occasionally including praise songs sung in other languages in your worship services. Most Christian music publishers sell sheet music and CDs with translations of hymns and praise songs. You can also find translations of popular songs along with worship songs from different regions of the world on the following Web sites:

- www.songsofpraise.org/translations.htm
- www.disciplethenations.org/index64.html
- www.ylw.mmtr.or.jp/~johnkoji/hymn/
- www.multilingual-southasian.com/pages/hindi/songs/hindisongs.htm
- www.integritymusic.com/espanol/nuestros_productos.htm

11. The world at your doorstep

If your church is near a university, you have the world at your doorstep! International students at colleges and universities come from a wide variety of cultural and religious backgrounds. Some are from countries closed to missionaries. Your community might also include immigrants or refugees. Just do a little research—you might be surprised to discover people from a variety of cultures living right next door.

A great way to reach out to international students and immigrants is by coordinating a monthly or bimonthly international dinner. Invite internationals to attend this potluck meal, and have congregation members supply the food. Do your best to sustain a one-to-one ratio of internationals and church members. Have church members sit with international students or immigrants and simply focus on developing friendships by asking questions about the guests' homelands, families, and interests. At each meal, include a short devotion or Bible story as well as a prayer. Non-Christian international students and immigrants will likely be interested in learning about Christianity in this nonthreatening setting simply because it's an important part of our culture. As church members build relationships with internationals over time, they'll have additional opportunities to tell others about Jesus.

12. Buttons and bows for needy babies

Coordinate a churchwide "baby shower" and ask church members to donate clothing and other items for mission agencies that primarily minister to young children and orphans in Third-World countries. Items such as bottles, cloth diapers, baby wipes, new infant and toddler clothing, blankets, diaper-rash ointment, and burp rags, toys, and teddy bears can help these children feel special and loved. Invite your congregation to bring their donated items on a specific Sunday, and take time during that morning's worship service to pray for the children who will receive the items and for the adults involved in the ministry to these children.

13. Taste of missions festival

Many big cities have a "Taste of [name of city]" summer festival where local restaurants set up booths. Participants can sample a variety of foods from the city's best eateries. Transform this concept into a fun family-oriented "Taste of Missions" celebration for your church. Invite volunteers to adopt specific regions of the world; learn about that region's culture, the spiritual climate there, what missionaries in that region are doing; and—most important—select and prepare a food item from that region (give each volunteer a photocopy of "8 Great Web Sites for Finding World Missions Information" on page 212). For your "Taste of Missions" night, volunteers will set up tables and distribute tastes of their food items. If necessary, charge a per-person fee to cover the cost of the food and let people roam through the festival and sample foods from different countries. Each time they visit a booth, participants should seek to learn about the region represented there.

As the evening winds down, gather participants together in an open area or in your church's worship area. Ask people to form groups of three, and have each trio discuss these questions:

- Which food was your favorite? Why?
- What was something new you learned today?
- What prayer needs stood out to you?
- How can our church do more to help people around the world learn about Jesus?

14 Creative Ways to Support Missionaries

Missionaries sacrifice a lot when they move halfway around the world. One thing they don't have to give up is fellowship with Christians back home. Of course, the people of your church can support missionaries by writing letters, giving money, and praying for missionaries. In addition to these three essentials, the following ideas can help your church family minister to missionaries and help them stay connected to home.

1. M.K. pen pals

Children's Sunday school classes can adopt one or more M.K.s (Missionary Kids) near their age. Each month, Sunday school teachers can arrange for their classes to create and send something to their M.K. pen pals. In addition to letters and e-mails, classes might send crayon self-portraits, homemade encouragement cards, sheets of stickers, craft supplies, homemade Christmas ornaments, a collection of kids' favorite Bible verses stapled together into a homemade book, or photographs of the class. Kids can also save money to buy something for their M.K. pen pals, such as a subscription to a Christian magazine for kids or teens, a fun board game, or a Christian CD. Missionary kids will feel special and loved as they develop new friendships with kids back at home!

2. Missions Central dot.com

Enhance your congregation's connection to and communication with your church-supported missionaries by creating a "Missions Central" page on your church's Web site. It can be the storehouse for all missions-related information the people of your church need in order to keep in touch with missionaries and develop a heart for world missions.

Recruit some tech-savvy members of your congregation to put the page together, with photos and bios of all the missionaries your church supports. Include updated facts about the work of the missionaries, as well as contact information and a link for e-mailing them. The Web page could also include newsletters missionaries send and specific prayer requests they want to share with your congregation. In addition, some mission agencies allow supporters to donate funds for specific missionaries via the Internet; if this applies to your church's missionaries, include links to these agency sites.

3. Mags in the mail

Collect recent Christian magazines from your church family, and recruit a volunteer to mail them to missionaries every few months. Missionaries will read them for their own encouragement and give them to other English-speaking friends as a tool for sharing Jesus' love.

4. Welcome-backpack

To welcome missionaries home for furlough—the extended period of time when they return to their home base for rest, fundraising, and training—have your church family put together a "Welcome Back" collection of gift certificates to local restaurants and grocery stores. Also suggest that the congregation create coupons for free services they can render. For example, qualified church members could donate services such as a haircut, a car wash, babysitting, lawn mowing, car tuneup, dental checkup, or tax help.

5. Missionary prayer shuffle

Encourage families in your congregation to start a collection of missionary prayer cards—those small cards that have a photo of the missionary family and information about where they serve. Encourage parents to teach their children the habit of praying for missionaries by playing a simple game. Each night at dinner, a different family member gets to shuffle the "deck" of prayer cards with his or her eyes closed. Your family then prays for the family whose card gets shuffled to the top that night.

6. Missionary movies

Invite missionary families to create short videos explaining what they do, showing their surroundings and some of the people they serve, and featuring their children. Have missionaries send their videos to your church, and show it to kids' Sunday school classes, complete with popcorn and drinks. Have Sunday school teachers lead kids in praying for the missionary they learned about. Give children the task of telling their parents what they learned and asking them to also pray for the missionary family.

7. 10 Most Wanted

Ask missionaries to send you a "10 Most Wanted" list—10 inexpensive pantry or household items that are hard to find where they live (such as a favorite chewing gum, peanut butter, a favorite brand of soap, or a specific type of lotion). Once you've collected a list from several missionary families, compile the list and print it in the church bulletin. Set out a sign-up sheet and donations box in the church foyer. Families in the church can sign up to purchase items from the list and drop them off in the donations box. Ask volunteers to package the items along with a note of encouragement, and then send them off to the various missionaries around the globe.

8. Keeping up with local news

If your church supports missionaries who are originally from your area, help them feel connected with happenings around the old hometown. Ask congregation members to read the local newspaper with these missionaries in mind. As they come across local news or feature stories, wedding announcements, obituaries, stories about changes in the town, or any other news items that might be of interest to missionaries, suggest that they cut out the articles. Remind them to send the clipped articles along with a note to the missionaries each month.

9. Prayer calendars

Create monthly calendars featuring a photo of a missionary family for each month. Most photo centers at grocery and drug stores offer this service. If your church supports fewer than 12 missionary families, include some families on more than one month. If the congregation supports more than 12 families, double up some months. Include the names and contact information for each missionary on their featured page. Distribute the calendars to members of your church. As they use the calendars to keep track of their own families' events, they can also pray for missionaries each day of the month.

10. Worship together across the globe

Invite tech-savvy, music-loving teenagers or college students to create CDs of popular worship music by purchasing (and we *do* mean "purchasing"!) and downloading songs from the Internet. Encourage them to choose songs that you regularly sing in your worship services, as well as other Christian songs they think missionaries or missionary kids would enjoy. Send the CDs to missionaries so they can hear the latest tunes from their favorite Christian artists during their personal times of worship.

11. Don't forget the extra suitcase

Whenever a team from your church takes a mission trip to a Third-World country, be sure to send an extra suitcase with the team. Several weeks before the trip, place the open suitcase in the church foyer and challenge the congregation to fill it with useful gifts the team can use for themselves or can give to the people they're ministering to. Church members might donate sample-sized toiletries such as toothpaste or deodorant, diapers and baby wipes, toothbrushes, packages of socks, combs, pens, and so on. The items in the extra suitcase will equip missionaries to minister to practical needs in small but important ways.

12. Let missionaries be ministered to

As a church, raise funds to send missionary couples to a spiritual retreat targeted to their needs. Many organizations host meaningful mini-sabbaticals for missionaries, spiritually refilling and strengthening them as they focus on their own walk with Jesus.

13. Stock their library

Around Christmastime, invite missionaries to create a wish list of books that could help them in their research, personal study, and ministry. Include the list in a church newsletter and ask church-family members to purchase and send these resources to the missionaries as Christmas gifts.

14. Furlough pantry party

Right before missionaries return home for furlough, host a "pantry party" at the church. Families from the church can bring nonperishable food items to fill the missionaries' pantry. This is especially fun when families include treats (like candy bars and soda) that will be a welcome sight to the eyes of missionary kids.